Nobody Much

Life on the Farm with Granny Cool

Barbara McIntyre

MADISON BOOKS
Lanham • New York • Oxford

First Madison Books edition 2003

Copyright © 2003 by Barbara McIntyre

All rights reserved
No part of this book may be reproduced in any form or by any electronic or mechanical means, including information storage and retrieval systems, without written permission from the publisher, except by a reviewer who may quote passages in a review.

Published by Madison Books
A Member of the Rowman & Littlefield Publishing Group
4501 Forbes Boulevard, Suite 200
Lanham, Maryland 20706

PO Box 317
Oxford
OX29RU, UK

Distributed by NATIONAL BOOK NETWORK

Library of Congress **Card Number: 2002115216**

ISBN 978-1-56833-254-3 (pbk.)

To Angus, who taught me to laugh; and to the kids, without whom there would be no story.

Acknowledgments

Thanks to Alan Williams, a former senior editor at Viking and longtime friend of my husband's, for being kind enough to get me headed in the right direction. Thanks to Annie, my screen writing daughter, who proofread my memoir from the family's point of view and kept me encouraged. Thanks to editor Alexandra Shelley, who proofread my memoir from an outsider's point of view and suggested many helpful changes. Thanks to Sue Mermelstein, copy editor for the New York Times, who cleaned up my punctuation and spelling. And particular thanks to my husband, Angus, who knowing my genius for technology, backed up my files, formatted the book on his computer and printed everything out more times than he cares to think about. Without all this support my memoir would have never seen the light of day.

Contents

Prologue ix

Part One

Meeting Nana 3
Moving to Dix Hills 15
Money, Babies, & Family 25

Part Two

Food 33
Tusie 43
The Decorators 57
Looking Good 67

Part Three

Life on the Farm: Horses and Holidays 79
Socializing 89
Sex, Marriage and Grandchildren 97

Part Four

Winding Down: The End of an Era 107

Prologue

This is a Long Island story. It's a story about the family I married into and the "farm" my children grew up on; but mostly it's a story about Margaret, my husband's stepmother, who married into the family a year before I did. She and Mac, my in-laws, came from Benton, Illinois, a small town down near the Kentucky border, and as far as I could see, they never got over it.

In a town like Benton, in the early 1900s, half the townsfolk were your relatives, the other half on a first-name basis, and a "private life" was an oxymoron. Neighbors knew each others' business as well as they knew their own. Margaret's mother, Maude Cantrell, could look out her living room window, pick up the phone and say to her neighbor, "Now, Grace, I don't think there's a thing in the world wrong, but I thought you ought to know that I just saw John come walking around the back of your house carrying a shotgun, and your Mary Lee was crying." By late afternoon everyone in town knew that Grace's son-in-law had threatened to kill himself and that his wife, Mary Lee, had cooled him down.

Benton developed in its citizenry a lifelong inquisitiveness, an insatiable curiosity about what was going on next door and around the corner. But at the same time it also bred a strong sense of family and place that tended to last forever. Like a bad cold, a Benton upbringing was hard to shake, its special brand of humor and inbred loyalty sticking stubbornly for the rest of one's life.

I never heard of Benton until I married my husband, and I never knew anyone else that had heard of it either. For years I wondered how one small town could have such a grip on the imaginations of the people who had once lived there that forever after it would define their lives. The one time I saw Benton, I found it in no way remarkable.

It seemed like any other small Midwestern town, with a variety of stores and municipal buildings around a central public square and neat close together houses lining Main Street. On the outskirts of town lay the farms and abandoned coal mines.

As it turned out, it had little to do with the town's appearance and everything to do with its townsfolk. Benton was an attitude, a way of dealing with the world, but most of all it was an attitude towards people.

By the time I met Margaret and Mac, at their place on Long Island in 1950, they had been gone from Benton for more than forty years. But from their conversation you would have thought they'd just left last week. Through the coal strikes and depressions, the wars and the unemployment, they had grown up laughing at life's ups and downs. Life goes better, they seemed to believe, when you don't take anything too hard.

When her housekeeper's husband was spotted on the South Shore of Long Island one day with the checkout girl from the A&P, Margaret never batted an eye. It just reminded her of that time long ago that *her* mother, in Benton, had a housekeeper by the name of Mrs. Shamus, a good woman who had the bad luck to catch her husband with his pants down.

Mrs. Shamus worked for Margaret's family six days a week, cleaning, washing and cooking. In the evening, after a long days' work, she bicycled home and cooked dinner again for her shiftless, out-of-work husband, Ed, and a lady boarder named Lily who'd recently moved in.

One Monday morning Mrs. Shamus arrived for work with a very large black eye.

"Why Mrs. Shamus, honey," cried Margaret's mother, "whatever in the world happened?"

"Well-l-l, you remember that lady boarder I was tellin' you about?" she drawled, hanging up her coat, "the one that recently moved in? I kinda suspected my Ed might be gettin' a little sweet on her." She blew her nose loudly. "So last week I kicked her out."

She let that sink in for a few moments and then continued. "I come home from church on Sunday and my Ed wasn't nowhere around. And I started thinkin', I'll bet he's with that woman. So I hopped on the train for West Frankfort, where I knew she was at, walked over to her apartment and knocked on the door."

"This voice said 'come in' so I went in, and there was my Ed, in bed with this woman."

"So I says, 'Well, hello Ed. Uh, who's that you got in bed with you?' and he kinda smiles and says 'Oh, nobody much!' and with that we went to fightin. And that's how I come by this here black eye!"

My mother-in-law, Margaret Cantrell McIntyre, would have been the first to admit that in the gallery of world players, she too was Nobody Much. But in the eyes of the only people whose opinion really mattered to her—her family and her eventual extended step-family, a group that included three stepchildren, their spouses and twelve step-grandchildren—she was right up there with Auntie Mame, Granny Cool, Ann Landers and the Mother Superior. She was irreverent and worldly and liked to tell us she'd "seen it all." After a life on the stage, she probably had. Nothing surprised her and she was impossible to fool.

When our exotic young Spanish-speaking neighbor left her husband and six children to accompany her stepfather on a three-week trip to South America one winter, ostensibly to serve as his interpreter, Margaret was the only one who smelled a rat. "Surely you didn't think that she was just going to translate, did you?" she asked us incredulously. And then she burst out laughing that anyone could be so naive. Sure enough, the marriage broke up shortly thereafter.

Margaret was an original all right, but stepmother and mother-in-law, two jobs with a lot of bad press, turned out to be right up her alley.

Nobody Much

PART ONE

Meeting Nana

ONE

I was listening to the new Speaker of the House, Newt Gingrich, rattling on and on about family values one night in 1995, not that long after Time magazine had named him Man of the Year and given him the mistaken impression he had the last word on everything. And it got me thinking it was too bad Nana wasn't around. She'd have set Newt straight on the whole subject. Family values was her field all right, she just never knew what it was called.

It never made the slightest difference to Nana whose family it was. Mac's family, my family, the cleaning woman's family or her hairdresser's family. As long as it was family, she wanted to get involved.

Like that morning Louetta, her longtime maid, arrived to clean her house. The first thing Nana asked her was how her sick brother was getting along. You'd have thought, listening to her carrying on, that it was Nana's own brother who had had the stroke, not Louetta's.

"Well... he's about same as he was last week," Louetta said, yanking the old Electrolux out of the cleaning closet. "He ain't better and he ain't worse." She gave the Electrolux a good kick and got it headed in the right direction. "Yesterday I was talkin' to the doctor at the hospital and he tells me there's but two kinds of strokes. One kind you gets better and the other you becomes a vegetarian."

"Is that right!" Nana said, a wicked gleam shining out of her light green eyes as she warmed to the subject. "Well, don't you worry Louetta, I'm sure your brother is going to be one of the ones that gets better and very soon. What are they planning to do to him next?"

"I thinks next week," said Louetta, "he goes into re-halibut-tation."

TWO

Nana was my mother-in-law. My stepmother-in-law. I called her Margaret, my children called her Nana and the help called her Nanner. Behind her back.

But I'm getting ahead of myself, because the first time I ever saw Margaret, I thought she was Louise. Same big face, same big nose, same reddish blond hair. Louise, the mother of an ex-boyfriend, was not one of my fans.

It was New York City, the winter of '49. "South Pacific" had opened on Broadway, Noel Coward's "Brief Encounter" was playing at the Washington Square Cinema Arts Theater, and if you were lucky enough to have a date, you met him under the clock at the Biltmore Hotel. Christian Dior was affecting the way American women dressed, and the stylish girls were wearing their skirts full and nearly to the ankle.

It was just before Christmas and the parties—the parties none of us had had during the war—were in full swing. One of my old beaux was back in town for the holidays and he'd invited me to a party on the top floor of a four-story walk-up right next to the Third Avenue El. I spied Margaret as soon as I walked in the door.

She was standing on the far side of a smokey room, crowded with recent college graduates, and I wondered what in the world Louise was doing at a party like this. Louise never went anywhere until she'd assured herself it was strictly top-drawer; and I couldn't figure out why someone pushing sixty would want to be at what was clearly a post-college bash, complete with beer kegs and pretzels.

I hadn't thought of Louise in months.

It was way last summer that she'd invited me to lunch one day at the Pierre, her favorite New York watering hole. Just me and Bill, her adored only child, whom I'd been dating on and off for the last year. Louise considered her Bill to be right up there with George Washington, Abraham Lincoln and the Holy Ghost; but her opinion of me wasn't all that clear.

I had just graduated from college and was working at my first job, and for lunch I was dressed in a black linen suit that had set me back three months' salary.

"Well," she said, giving me an air-kiss as she checked me up and down, "you're looking very well indeed. I hardly recognized you."

She turned and followed the headwaiter to our table, while I wondered if I'd been complimented or not. She always had a knack for making me feel ten years old again; I half expected to have to show her my fingernails were clean before I was allowed to eat.

We sat down at our table and I looked around the room. Everywhere were massive bouquets of lilacs, dogwood and pink tulips, and enough waiters to handle three more dining rooms. I settled back in my plush, overstuffed chair, warm with pleasure and expectation, and waited for lunch. This was not going to be my usual peanut butter sandwich on the fly. With a starting salary of $48.50 a week, the Pierre was as foreign to my lifestyle as a trip to Bali.

"Now," Louise said, patting my arm and staring inquisitively at the table next to us, "I want to hear all about your new job."

"Bill," she went on, turning to her son, "did I tell you that the Osbornes are coming to town next week? I don't think they've been out of St. Louis in twenty years. Lydia won some tickets to a Broadway show and she finally decided to lay down the law. She told Tom she was going to New York whether he liked it or not. And that if he didn't want to go, she'd find someone who did. I told her she should have done that years ago. *Years ago.* That he probably wouldn't have even known she was gone." She took a big sip of her very dry martini.

"Speaking of being gone, remember that time that Cousin Mary packed her bag and went to Chicago for three days and her husband didn't even know she'd left the house?" Louise and Bill both shook with laughter remembering Mary and emptied their drinks. I was already gaining insight into how people from Southern Illinois converse, even those who'd migrated to St. Louis, but at the time I just wondered who all these people were.

Louise waved her menu at our waiter and ordered two more martinis. She then patted my arm again. "What were we talking about? Oh yes dear, you were going to tell me all about your job."

For the last three months I had been working as a reporter for Eugenia Sheppard, who ran the Style page of the New York Herald Tribune. Though hardly a seasoned veteran of the fashion wars, I had in no time at all become outspokenly opinionated about the whole industry.

What, Louise asked, looking directly at me for the first time, now that she'd satisfied herself there was no one else important in the room, did I think of Mademoiselle magazine for instance?

Mademoiselle was a fairly recent entry in the magazine field and to my mind had not as yet found its voice. In my newfound wisdom, I felt it was rather slipshod and poorly put together, not very interesting and certainly no Vogue. I thought a moment, searching for the right word, and finally said, "Well, I think it's really a crappy magazine."

A loud honking noise emanated from Bill as he pretended to sneeze. Louise studied the chives in her vichyssoise as though they had suddenly grown roots.

The silence, as they say, was deafening, the only sounds in the room coming from the other tables.

Finally Louise let out a very long breath and said, "You know, that's really not a proper word for a nice young lady like yourself to use." This was, after all, still the forties, not that long since Rhett Butler had sworn at Scarlett O'Hara and caused a nationwide uproar. She didn't have to add, because the implication was instantly clear, that I wasn't proper marriage material for the Holy Ghost either.

The conversation limped on from there but it never fully recovered. And needless to say, neither did the relationship with Bill. What I neglected to tell her was that I hadn't the faintest idea what the word really meant. I thought it meant sloppy, not very well done.

That night when I got home I called Robby. I'd known Robby since kindergarten and I could always count on him to fill in the gaps. He knew what "copulation" meant in the third grade, even though he couldn't spell it till the seventh.

"Crappy? It has to do with feces." I didn't know what feces meant either but I was beginning to get the general idea. "There's another word that's considered even worse than crap, but for the time being you'd probably better skip them both."

Anyway, there I was at that Christmas party the winter of 1949, and there was Margaret when I thought she was Louise. I went up and introduced myself.

"It's the funniest thing," I said, "but you look just like someone I know. In fact that's who I thought you were when I first saw you." I went on to tell her Louise's name and that I used to date her son.

"Well that is pretty funny," she replied laughing, "because Louise just happens to be my first cousin and I've known her son since the day he was born." I smiled weakly at her through my astonishment and drifted away, praying my reputation hadn't preceded me.

I still couldn't figure out what Margaret was doing at this party. Wall-to-wall young people, inhaling beer and listening to the Third Avenue El thundering by outside, hardly seemed her scene. The noise level inside was deafening. Every time a train rolled by, the windows rattled and the lamps lurched. You had to shout to make yourself heard but nobody seemed to mind; it all just contributed to the general air of hilarity.

I figured she must be at least thirty years older than everyone else in the room, maybe more, but she was obviously having as good a time as anyone, chatting easily with people a generation younger.

"Who is that woman over there?" I said, pointing at Margaret. "She's very charming—actually at first I thought she was someone else." I was talking to a young man I had just met. He was tall and skinny, with hair that had already started to go grey, and he seemed to know everybody there.

He followed my finger over to the corner where Margaret was laughing, and said, "That's my stepmother, Margaret McIntyre. My sister, Sally Lewis, is giving the party, and she thought she'd enjoy it. My father doesn't go to parties if he can possibly avoid it. Besides he'd never make it up four flights of stairs with his bad legs. By the way, I'm Angus McIntyre, who are you?"

Six months later I was his wife and Margaret McIntyre was my stepmother too. My stepmother in-law, that is. And if you think you know all about stepmothers, think again.

I never knew another soul who had an ex-Ziegfeld Follies singing star for a mother-in-law. And that's just for starters.

THREE

But I'm getting ahead of myself again, because the next time I saw Margaret, months before she was my mother-in-law, was on Long Island. I'd been invited home for the weekend to Meet The Family.

Meeting The Family is a stomach cruncher in anyone's book. Still, Angus had talked so much about the "gentleman's farm" where he'd been born and raised that I was curious to see it. I knew the farm was somewhere in the middle of the island but I didn't know exactly where. Long Island to me meant the Hamptons, where I had summered growing up. The rest of the island, as far as I was concerned, was simply the way you got there.

I knew that Margaret had moved into the Big House after her marriage to Mac the previous year, and that Angus' brother and sister, both married, continued to live there in cottages. What I couldn't understand is why the young marrieds would still be hanging around. To me the best part of getting married was moving on.

Late one Friday afternoon towards the end of February, Angus picked me up at work and headed east to the Northern State Parkway. A little over an hour later, we turned off at Huntington and headed south.

Outside it was cold and dark, with a light dusting of snow on the frozen ground. The narrow backcountry roads, unlit by any street lamps, seemed as remote as Greenland. If there were any neighbors around, they were all but invisible. I pulled my thin wool coat tighter around me, wishing I'd left my city clothes in New York.

The farm, I assumed, must be large, since I understood there was a colonial house, a stable, a swimming pool, two cottages and assorted barns and outbuildings; but that night as we drove down the long driveway, I don't remember noticing a single thing. All I could think about was what everyone would think of me.

The family was gathered around the fireplace waiting impatiently for us to arrive. So as soon as we'd taken off our coats and tidied up, we went directly into dinner.

We all took our places around a mahogany dining room table, bright with pink linen place mats and silver candelabra, and waited for dinner to be served.

At one end of the table sat Mac, whom I was meeting for the first time, and at the end nearest the kitchen, Margaret. In between sat Angus' brother, Ranny, and his wife, Helen (pregnant with their first child); his sister, Sally Lewis and her husband, Taf (who had given the Christmas party in their four-story walk-up); and Angus and me. A lone blonde in a sea of brunettes. Margaret picked up a small silver bell in front of her and rang it.

Through the pantry door burst Agnes, a lantern-jawed Swedish woman built like a refrigerator and puffing like a terminal asthmatic. She was carrying a serving platter on which an enormous pork roast ringed with browned potatoes teetered precariously.

Margaret helped herself to a large piece of meat and two potatoes and attacked her dinner. I was served next; and after helping myself, wondered what to do. My conventional Westchester family, more hung up on the proper way of doing things than the why of doing things, had insisted that no one eat until everyone at the table had been served. I decided to wait and see what the next person did.

"Where did you grow up, Bobbie?" Margaret asked, chewing a piece of pork and helping herself to a biscuit.

"In Scarsdale," I said, not touching my food.

My family had also insisted we not talk with our mouths full.

"But my freshman year in college, my mother moved to New York. My father died just before the war; and with my sister and brother and me all away at school, she felt the house was too big and too lonely."

"Does your mother like it in New York?" Margaret went on, putting three string beans on her plate and buttering two more biscuits.

"I guess now that she was alone she thought life would be more fun in the city than in the suburbs. There'd be more people to meet, more things to do. She bought the house in Bridgehampton about the same time, so she'd have a place to go in the summer."

"How did you get the job with the Tribune?" Margaret asked. "That sounds like fun. Agnes," she yelled towards the kitchen, "bring some gravy. Honestly, what in the world do you suppose she's doing in there?"

"Well, my father had been in the advertising business and someone at his company knew the head of personnel at the Trib. The personnel director sent me to see Eugenia and Eugenia gave me a chance."

Everyone seemed to want to hear more about the Tribune and about Eugenia, so I launched into a rather lengthy discussion of what it was like to work at a newspaper, who was in the fashion department and where I had learned to type.

Along with the writing of the occasional human interest story, my daily assignment was to attend fashion shows and showroom exhibitions and then return to the paper and write a short piece describing what I had seen. The following day the story ran under my byline, a heady trip for a recent Smith graduate who had slid through academia more focused on the curriculum extracurricular than the one I was paying for.

Eugenia was an indulgent and forgiving boss. Small and doll-like, with wide china blue eyes, she had a deceptively demure appearance; underneath that soft mass of girlishly curled white hair, lay a very sharp lady.

In her heart she thought the fashion world was vain and silly, and like many newspaper editors her copy usually had a sly edge to it. Unlike the magazine ladies, she refused to take the fashion business too seriously, and felt she owed it to her readers to let them in on the joke. Her only concession to how she looked herself was that she usually wore some shade of blue to complement her eyes.

Like all good editors she cut me a lot of slack and occasionally I hung myself. Once, when I attended a summer fashion show held outdoors under a large tent at Gracie Mansion, I came back to write that the day had been warm and delightful, the clothes sublime and we had all sat under a canape. Eugenia just cleaned up my spelling and sent it in.

"I just love Eugenia," laughed Margaret "I always read her, she's so entertaining. She should write a gossip column, don't you think?" She paused for a moment and looked at my plate.

"Don't you like your dinner, Bobbie?" she asked.

I glanced around the table and to my chagrin saw that everyone had finished their meals. Seven empty plates stared back at me. I hadn't even begun.

I suppose to give me a chance to eat, someone asked Mac to tell a story. So far he hadn't said a word. It seemed to be what he was waiting for, as he brightened almost immediately. I quit talking and started eating, sure that like the big dustup with Louise, I had already said too much.

Mac began a long tale that I could barely follow, something about a man throwing a lady's noisy toy poodle out the window of a moving train in Southern Illinois. In retaliation, the woman then grabbed the man's pipe and threw it out the window. While they were bad-mouthing each other, they looked out the window and down the track came the poodle with the pipe in his mouth. It was a true story and there was probably a lot more to it than that, but that was the general idea.

I could see that Mac enjoyed telling stories; I could also see that he was used to being the center of attention. No sooner had he begun talking than everyone started to smile. Pretty soon they were all chuckling. Clearly this was a very familiar story, but that just seemed to make it all the funnier.

By the time he had finished, everyone was laughing out loud, Margaret was saying "Oh, Mac, honestly" and I was wondering what all the commotion was about. I couldn't imagine why anyone would laugh at a story he'd heard so many times.

I smiled politely and finished my dinner. I didn't think the story was funny at all.

During dessert the conversation turned to feminine beauty, with a lot of sanctimonious talk about how the natural look was so much more attractive. "I don't think Sophie Wilson is pretty at all," someone said about a flamboyant family friend. "She wears make-up all the time."

"Well, we wouldn't know anything about that, would we, Bobbie?" said Margaret, laughing and looking right at me.

I could see that Margaret, who I knew had been on the stage, wore make-up, but I couldn't believe she noticed it on me. For years I had been darkening my pale eyelashes, the downside of being blond, but I was sure my guilty little secret was undetectable. In 1950, except for a little lipstick, no one but movie stars and hookers used make-up.

I pretended I hadn't heard her and thought longingly of the city.

The next morning when I still hadn't appeared by 11:00, Agnes was sent upstairs to wake me. The early rising family assumed that anyone who slept past 7:30, even on a weekend, was either terminally lazy or must have died in her sleep.

Agnes banged into my room with a cup of coffee the consistency of mud, yanked my hair and said, "Good morning, Miss Bobbie, time to get up now." Then she went out and slammed the door.

I could hardly wait to get back to New York.

Somehow or other during the ensuing months, the specter of the farm, the family and the formidable Agnes retreated into the background. Angus and I continued to see each other in New York and Bridgehampton, and by July when we decided to get married, I simply assumed we would be living in New York.

I couldn't think of anything more fun than being young and in love and living in New York.

On a hot sticky day towards the end of August, Angus and I were married in my mother's Bridgehampton garden. The night before, at the Post House in Southampton, where Mac threw a bridal dinner, my younger brother asked Margaret to dance. She said it was the first time anyone had danced with her in more than twenty-five years.

FOUR

It was around 9:00 Saturday morning and Angus and I were having our usual weekend argument. We had only been married a short time but already the question of how we spent our weekends had become an ongoing issue. As I rolled over to my side of the bed, the phone started to ring.

"You get it," I said, burying my head in the pillow. I knew it would be Margaret wanting to know if we were coming to the country for dinner and right now I didn't want to think about it. I didn't see why we had to go out to the Place, as the family called the farm they had owned since the twenties, every single weekend. I could think of hundreds of things to do in the city; in the country there was nothing to do except eat and throw walnuts for the dogs.

I loved the city. I loved our cozy little apartment in Gramercy Square. I loved going to the small local restaurants for dinner with my brand new husband, especially on weekends when he wasn't rushed. And I loved the new art-film theaters that had sprung up like weeds all over town.

My idea of a perfect Saturday was a late afternoon movie, preferably British, and a long, leisurely meal afterwards, preferably French. Funny and irreverent, Angus, I was discovering, could and would hold forth interminably on almost any subject, whether he knew anything about it or not, and a restaurant was his favorite forum. Besides, what new bride wants to spend every weekend with her in-laws?

Angus was sounding cordial and cheerful, an ominous sign. He was sounding like someone who was planning to go to the country.

"We're just waking up," he stalled, looking over at me and recognizing intransigence when he saw it. "Can we get back to you? Yes, sure, a pork roast would be just fine. Well, I don't know if Bobbie's ever had a peach cobbler."

Three hours later we were headed over the 59th Street bridge for Long Island and I was still complaining.

"The main reason Margaret wants us out there, you know, is so she can plan a big meal," I said. "Eating is what it's all about. It really is. I wouldn't care if I never *saw* another pork roast." Angus smiled and pointed out some locust trees on a hill by the road where he used to go horseback riding, and changed the subject.

We took our time getting out of the city, stopping along the way to eat lunch and look at antiques, and finally drove into the Place around mid-afternoon. It was early October and the aging maple trees that lined the long driveway had already started to yellow. The lovely old white colonial house at the top of the rise and the sweeping lawn leading up to it glowed in the soft fall light. I had to admit that the country had its advantages, but I certainly had no wish to ever live on a family compound. Who wants in-laws breathing down one's neck?

If we ever did decide to live in the country, which we might when we had children, we most certainly would find our own place. Perhaps a house over on the North Shore where we knew some people. Somewhere nearer the water. I had discovered that not only did I not know anyone in the area but neither did anyone else. If it was a social life I was yearning for, the neighboring vegetable farms and wholesale nurseries were not going to be much help.

We parked our secondhand Ford convertible down by the garage and walked up the long bluestone path to the house. As the front door opened, I was enveloped in a miasma of simmering pork roast and fried onions.

"Hi," I yelled at Margaret and Mac, who were sitting happily in front of the fire, reading and drinking coffee. "Be with you in a minute." I ran up the stairs to our bedroom, leaned over the toilet and threw up.

Nine months later our son, Sandy, was born and I too was living on the family place in the middle of Long Island. My education in family living, Southern Illinois style, had begun.

Moving to Dix Hills

ONE

A few months ago Angus and I were at a dinner party in Locust Valley and it happened again. Someone I'd never met before asked me where I lived. Ordinarily this is not a subject that causes anyone too much agitation. But for me, explaining where I live has always been a sore point.

I'd never heard of Dix Hills until one day about twenty years ago the Post Office sent me a letter saying that's where I lived. Never mind that for the twenty-five years before that, the family compound that I call home had been located in the township of Huntington.

Huntington has gotten too big, said the Post Office in its infinite wisdom, and from now on you live in Dix Hills, even though you haven't moved, and even though you're still in exactly the same place. The thing to understand here is that given the pack I run with, Dix Hills has never been what you'd call a social asset. My friends tend to think of it with the same mind set as, say, Tibet or the Outer Hebrides.

Locust Valley, Oyster Bay, Cold Spring Harbor, even Huntington. All okay. North Shore Long Island. But Dix Hills?

"So where exactly is Dix Hills?" said my dinner partner, one of those sleek North Shore types with marbles in his mouth and little velvet slippers on his feet.

"It's south of Jericho Turnpike."

"Where?" he repeated, not sure he'd heard me right, his face wearing the same expression I use sometimes when I get downwind of my dog.

"Well, actually it's south of the Long Island Expressway."

He stared at a spot somewhere to the left of my nose for a minute and then attacked his chicken cutlet. It was clear he had concluded that Dix Hills must be somewhere in the Bronx.

Our North Shore friends have repeatedly gotten lost coming to our house for dinner. Some have made it clear that their visit to Dix Hills was a onetime trauma they'd just as soon forget. To tell the truth the only reason that 120 people showed up for our daughter Katy's wedding (and this despite the fact that the Long Island weather was so bad that the county of Queens received federal disaster funds) is that every guest had a detailed map giving a choice of at least six routes. It was our biggest social triumph, if what you're counting are sheer numbers. But more about that later.

Moving to Dix Hills never bothered Margaret at all. Born and raised in Benton, a town she left at the age of 18, she had spent her whole working life either in New York City or touring with the road company of "The Student Prince". The day she married Mac and became a country housewife, she simply exchanged one telephone number for another.

In the mornings, she'd call her cousin Tusie, or her cousin Vivian, or her cousin Louise. In the afternoon she'd call her mother or her ex-sister-in-law, who were both still in Benton. And evenings, if Mac was out of town, she'd call her old friend Eleanor, who lived in Greenwich and slept until noon. If she needed to see someone, she'd visit her new stepchildren.

As far as living in Dix Hills was concerned, Margaret didn't know Dix Hills from Massapequa. It was all Long Island to her. Country or city, it made no difference; she could keep in touch with family from anywhere.

TWO

How the family came to settle in Dix Hills was pure happenstance.

Mac, my father-in-law, left Benton in his early twenties. Smart, handsome and charismatic, he was a young man in a hurry, eager to put some distance between himself and small town life.

No one ever knew for sure whether he went to college; but if he did go, it was only briefly. He was a prodigious reader and a quick study, and he was dead certain he could do anything he set his mind to.

Almost immediately, he got a job selling coal. Working the territory between North and South Dakota, two of the coldest places on earth, he quickly discovered he was a natural born salesman. His boss said he could have sold coal to the Mexicans in July.

Next, wending his way eastward, he talked himself into a job with Sears, Roebuck in Chicago, writing copy for its mail order catalogue and answering customer correspondence. He had never written any copy before.

Copy writing he found entertaining. It was creative and he had a talent for it. But replying to disgruntled customers was another story.

One day a long diatribe arrived in the mail from an angry customer in Dearborn, Michigan. Among other things the letter said, "What kind of a cheap two-bit outfit is Sears, Roebuck anyway? I just received the stove I ordered from you people and no one bothered to include the legs. I'd like to know how in the world I'm supposed to use a stove that hasn't any legs without setting my whole house on fire. I'm never going to buy anything from your lousy rotten company again." Signed, "Yours truly, Ezra Martin." And then, "P.S. I found the goddamn legs in the packing."

Another time, a letter came from a man who said he understood Sears, Roebuck sold a special kind of telescope, which if you stood outside and looked through it, you could see what was going on in the upstairs window of the house across the street. He said he'd like to buy one, since he'd become very interested in the woman who lived there.

Of course no such telescope existed, but rather than let the gentleman down gently, one burnt-out employee shot back, "You old fool, do you think if we had such a thing we'd *sell* it?"

Before long Mac got himself hired by Charles Williams Stores, a start-up company in Brooklyn, who made him an offer he couldn't refuse. It asked him to create a mail order catalogue that would compete directly with Sears and it asked him to do it in New York.

By the time he arrived in New York in his early thirties, he'd already acquired some of the trappings of success. He'd bought a Buick roadster with a rumble seat, a horse that he stabled in Jamaica, Queens, and a wardrobe of elegant clothes. His shoes and shirts sported English labels and his suits were being custom made.

Not knowing the area, he at first rented an apartment. But he also began thinking seriously about putting down roots. A big place in the country was what he had in mind, a place where you could raise a family. In particular, he wanted a place large enough to keep horses.

In due course he drove the Buick out to Long Island one day, and without too much thought, bought forty overgrown acres with a down-at-the-heels house, an even shabbier cottage and some decrepit outbuildings. No one had lived there for years and he was able to buy it all for less than $10,000. It was the kind of place that realtors always describe as "Needs Work."

The day he bought the farm, he had no idea where the preferred sections to live on the island were and made no effort to find out. Had he tried to buy on the North Shore, Long Island's Gold Coast, he would have found it way beyond his means. Mac wanted to live to the manor born, but he didn't get it quite right. He ended up with his beautiful country place on the wrong side of the tracks. The forty-acre farm he bought, which he eventually expanded to seventy-five, turned out to be in the southernmost part of Huntington township, smack in the middle of the Island, a truck farming area that eventually became known as Dix Hills. It was never fashionable and probably never would be; but by the time he found that out, he couldn't have cared less.

He came to take a perverse pleasure in living out of the loop, the social ramble never having been his scene anyway. When people asked him, as they inevitably did, if he lived near the water, he bragged that he was about as far from the water as you could get. On all sides.

About the same time that he bought the farm, he met and married Virginia Pomeroy, a tall, striking Bryn Mawr graduate from Minneapolis who was working in New York. A mutual friend who knew they were both from the Midwest introduced them.

The summer following their wedding, they lived in a tent on the front lawn of their farm, while the down-at-the-heels house was made fit to live in.

THREE

Margaret left Benton even earlier, sometime in her teens, her eyes firmly focused on studying voice and pursuing a career on the stage. Married life was at the bottom of her agenda.

She and Mac had known each other as children; but their lives never came together again until Margaret was in her late fifties, her career on the stage long over, and Mac was in his sixties, a lonely widower on Long Island with three grown children desperate to sort out his life.

Mac was a man with very few domestic talents. He could ride a horse, train a hunting dog and tell funny stories, but his cooking skills consisted of making coffee in his bedroom at 3:30 in the morning when he couldn't sleep. He drank so much coffee it didn't wake him up even at 3:30 in the morning and it certainly didn't help him sleep. It just tasted good when he was bored and restless and tired of lying in bed.

Anyway, he couldn't sleep most of the time, he didn't know how to cook, he was depressed that he was suddenly alone and something had to be done.

So one day, Angus and his brother, Ranny, who were both still pursuing their G.I. Bill undergraduate degrees at Yale (but had come home for the weekend to check on their father), picked up the phone and called Margaret Cantrell in New York City. Was there any chance she might like to come out for the weekend? She would indeed. Why didn't she catch the 5:00 train, they said, and someone would pick her up.

It was relaxed and easy having Margaret visit. She and Mac had known each other all their lives after all; and as part of the old Benton crowd who regularly kept in touch, Margaret had known Virginia and Mac's children as well.

Before long, Margaret was a regular fixture on weekends; and it wasn't too long afterward that she and Mac decided to marry. There was no reason not to. It suited everyone.

She quit her job as a receptionist at the Avco Corporation, one of the many jobs she had held since her career on the stage had ended, and terminated the lease on her small apartment. When I met her at Sally's party, that Christmas of '49, she was 57 years old and had been married for less than a year. It was her first and only marriage.

FOUR

"So how come Margaret never got married before?"

It was Sunday morning in New York not long after we were married, and Angus and I were lying lazily in bed talking. I was eager to keep the conversation going so that the back rub he was giving me wouldn't stop. Pregnancy was making me uncomfortable and back rubs provided a welcome relief.

All those years she was on the stage, he said, she'd never wanted to quit. First it was "The Student Prince", a popular operetta by Sigmund Romberg, which opened in 1924 and played for almost two years, and then it was the Ziegfeld Follies.

"I can't remember whether she sang the lead role in "The Student Prince" or just had a featured role, but I know she sang the lead role of Kathie in the touring company. In the Follies she was a showgirl, but she also got to sing again. You can't imagine how exciting it was for a small town girl from Benton, Illinois, to be on the New York stage."

The folks back home were thrilled, he went on. Those who could afford it came to New York to catch the show; others heard about it secondhand. One way or another everyone in town knew that Margaret Cantrell, Maude and George Cantrell's daughter, was singing on Broadway. They even knew about the night Flo Ziegfeld hired her.

Florenz Ziegfeld was a short, randy theatrical producer in his late fifties who had a passion for tall, toothsome young women, preferably stacked. He always made it a point to personally interview all potential showgirls. He had called Margaret back for a third interview, only this time he told her to come in the evening, not in the morning like the first two.

"Come in," he said warmly, opening the door to his private office. It was after 9:30 and everyone else had gone home. He closed the door, turned and smiled, and in an instant was after her, chasing her around and around and around his large mahogany desk. But despite her high heels and her too tight dress, Margaret managed to stay just out of reach. Eventually Ziegfeld got so winded, he gave up, but since it was late and he was tired, he gave her the job anyway.

After the Follies had been running for several months, Margaret's parents, Maude and George Cantrell, came to New York to catch the show. Margaret had reserved seats for them ten rows from the center of the stage.

In the second act, followed by a line of dancers, Margaret came out singing. "Hold me in your loving arms," she warbled, unaware that as she strolled around the stage, the train from her dress was slowly winding itself around her legs. As her movements became more and more constricted, one of the dancers spotted the gathering problem.

In an inspired bit of improvisation, he led a wholly unchoreographed dance around and around her as each dancer dipped down, one after the other, to disentangle the mess. As the last wrap was finally unwound, the song ended, and the whole theater burst into wild applause as Margaret sauntered off the stage.

"Margaret, honey," her father said later, "you were wonderful, the absolute hit of the show." George and Maude had gone backstage after the finale to greet their daughter and meet the cast. "And weren't those dancers clever? But, Margaret, there's just one thing Momma and I want to know: do you think that any of those fellas up there were *curious*?"

I laughed at the Benton expression for "gay" and told Angus to keep rubbing. "So then what?"

"Well, eventually she couldn't sing on the stage anymore and she started playing the piano and singing in speakeasies. It was Prohibition then and midtown New York was filled with illegal saloons looking for entertainment. You know, when she was a young girl, growing up in Benton, she played the piano in her parents' movie house for the silent films. So playing in a speakeasy wasn't all that different. She knew all the songs by heart, and what's more she could play them in the dark.

"I remember she told about one interview she went on at the Blue Note Café. She took her cousin Tusie's young son, George Boone, who couldn't have been more than thirteen at the time. I suppose she took him for protection; she didn't want to get chased around anyone's desk again; but by this time she was also funny about telling her age. If anyone asked her how old she was, she'd say 39. 'If they laughed, I laughed,' she explained. 'If they didn't, I didn't.' Anyway, the owner looked at George and said, 'Is this your son?' 'No,' said Margaret, 'It's my little brother.'"

Angus rolled over and said his arm was about to drop off and how about my rubbing his back for a while. I said okay, and he said he was sick of talking.

Later, over a late breakfast, the subject came up again. "So what happened after her speakeasy days?" I asked. I thought Angus had had enough coffee to get on with it.

"Well, eventually Prohibition got repealed by Roosevelt in 1933 and her speakeasy days ended. She played piano in cocktail lounges for a while and then I think she got a job at Elizabeth Arden, selling stuff behind the counter." He started laughing.

"I remember she told us that one day the Countess de Rothschild came in and struck up a conversation with her. She'd only been working for about a week. I guess Margaret was known for her beautiful skin. In any case the Countess was staring at her intently. 'My deah,' said the Countess in her deep throaty voice, putting on her glasses, 'have you had a peeling?' Peelings were a new service that Arden had just started offering and the Countess was thinking of having one. 'No," Margaret said, 'I haven't, but I definitely plan to next week!'"

"How long did she stay at Elizabeth Arden?" I asked.

"Not very long, I don't think. She kept getting in trouble. One day Miss Arden came in and looking right at Margaret, whom she'd never seen before, said, 'What's that and how much is it?' She was pointing at a small plastic case that was sitting on the counter."

"'That's a beach bag and it costs $25,' answered Margaret. It was an airplane bag and it cost $125."

"'Get rid of her,' said Miss Arden, to no one in particular."

About this time, Angus continued, Margaret was sharing an apartment with her old friend Muriel, whom she'd known on the stage. Muriel was between marriages and living on $50 a month alimony. Her wealthy sportsman husband, whom she'd married when she was young and pretty, had moved on to someone younger and prettier, leaving Muriel with her greying hair, her sagging jowls and her drooping eyes to make the best of it.

One day Margaret was stopped by Sheila, her boss at Arden's, and asked if she knew anyone they could test a new product on for a few weeks. The product was Firmalift, and it was highly touted as tightening the skin.

A few days later, Margaret brought in some pictures of Muriel to show to Sheila who said with delight that she was a perfect candidate. Just about everything sagged. When Miss Arden saw the pictures she agreed. "She looks just like a hound dog," she said.

Sheila gave Margaret two jars of Firmalift to take home and for three weeks just before going to bed Muriel carefully slathered the cream all over her face.

At the end of the three weeks Margaret took some new pictures of Muriel to compare with the ones she'd taken at the beginning and took them to Sheila. In the "before" pictures, her whole face drooped. Just as Margaret took out the "after" pictures to show Sheila, Miss Arden walked up to have a look.

"She still looks like a hound dog," Miss Arden screamed, and slapped Sheila right over Margaret's head.

"After Margaret left Arden's," Angus went on, "I forget what she did, but the jobs kind of wound down from there and she eventually ended up as a receptionist at Avco. That's what she was doing when Daddy came into the picture. I think at that point she was more than happy to quit working and do something different with her life. She was, after all, 56 years old, and had been working on and off her whole life."

Money, Babies & Family

ONE

So here I was in the summer of 1952 doing what I said I'd never do. I was living on a family compound in the middle of nowhere, up to my eyeballs in family values. To say I was apprehensive was putting it mildly. Living next door to my mother-in-law, I figured, would just be my mother times ten. Besides, I hated horses.

It was my pregnancy that propelled us out of the city. Angus and I both agreed that a New York apartment was no place to raise kids, and I had finally caved in on the subject of Living on the Place. This was one argument, I realized, I was never going to win.

There was only one hitch. All the houses were taken. Angus' brother, Ranny, and his wife, Helen, were living in the white cottage near the Big House; and his sister, Sally, and husband, Taf, were living in the red cottage on Half Hollow Road.

On a cold rainy day we went looking for a house site, found a spot high on a hill where a small apple tree had decided to grow and called a builder. To the family's astonishment, we put up a house of wood, stone and glass, as modern in feel as the others were old. It was finished three weeks before our son, Sandy, was born.

I'd been assuming that since Angus' brother and sister were both living in free cottages, Mac would of course pay for our house too. Anyone with as much money as he obviously had could easily afford it.

But as it turned out, I couldn't have been more mistaken. On all counts.

TWO

By the time I met Mac in 1950, his dream of a patrician lifestyle had become a reality. He had a cook, a cleaning woman, a chauffeur and two gardeners. He had seventy-five acres bordered by post and rail fences; a stable with a tack room, a hayloft, and ten stalls; an Olympic-size swimming pool and pool house; a vegetable garden in the apple orchard near the house; perennial borders on the lawn next to the house; and horses grazing in the two outer fields. I knew nobody had a lifestyle like that without money, but I hadn't a clue where the money had come from.

Money was a subject I knew almost nothing about. Growing up I had accepted my father's dictum that it was bad manners to ask how much anything cost and had arrived at young adulthood blissfully ignorant of the realities of life.

But I was beginning to think that money was the last great secret. Put people on prime time television and you'll hear more than you ever cared to about their dysfunctional children, their deteriorating health and their kinky sex lives; but ask them how much money they have and they clam right up.

I was learning, too, that appearances are often misleading. Some people flaunt what they have, some hide it. Every day you read about some poor soul that lived in a five-story walk-up, ate Fancy Feast for dinner, and then left ten million dollars to an alma mater that can't even remember him.

The first time I saw the farm, I simply assumed that Mac had money. If this wasn't the way rich people lived, what was?

Well, it was and it wasn't. Everyone in the neighborhood thought that Mac was wealthy, but the truth was more complex.

Over the years, ever since he'd bought the farm in the 1920s, Mac's income had mirrored the times. He had had as many ups and downs as a market graph. If the economy was strong, he made money; if the job market evaporated, he didn't. With no inherited wealth to fall back on, he had little cushion against adversity. His salary (or the lack of it) was the family's main support.

During the Depression, and long after, while others jumped out windows and put bullets through their brains, Mac sold eggs, milk and produce from the farm. That, combined with a monthly check from his first wife's banker father, was enough to get by. It wasn't gracious living, but selling the Place or getting rid of the horses was never even an option.

In the 1940s, his fortunes changed dramatically. Reuben H. Donnelley, a large direct marketing firm, hired him to sell advertising at 10 percent commission; before long, he was earning more money than the president and ready to branch out on his own. By the time he married Margaret in 1948, his own company had been running a year.

It was a competing direct marketing firm named O.E. McIntyre, Inc. and his original clients were three A-list companies he took with him from Donnelley: Readers Digest (which was also an investor), Time-Life and Meredith Publishing. That same year he also persuaded his two sons, Ranny and Angus, to join him. When I met Angus, the Christmas of '49, he was already commuting to Montreal and Toronto to start the Canadian branch of the business.

For the first time in years, there was enough money to fix up the place, enough to hire help, enough to live like the landed gentry Mac had had in mind in the first place.

Well, sort of.

He hired two brothers named Vinny and Ray to work on the grounds; he hired a groom named Jimmy to take care of the horses; he hired a chauffeur named Ed to drive him to work; and he put them all on the company payroll. He then had the company buy him a Cadillac for the chauffeur to drive and rent him an apartment in the city, in case he didn't feel like commuting.

It was an elegant lifestyle all right, but most of it was done with smoke and mirrors.

To her everlasting relief, Margaret's marriage coincided with the good times. No one ever had less interest in doing housework, cooking meals, washing dishes or digging in the garden. As for driving herself anywhere, three miles down the road to the A&P and her hairdresser was as far as she wanted to venture.

As she said to her young friend George, when she bumped into him at a party several years after her wedding, "Isn't it great, George, that we both married rich?!"

So as it turned out, thanks to the mortgage department of the Industrial Bank of Commerce, which was also bankrolling the growing McIntyre company, we paid for the house ourselves.

THREE

Between 1950 and 1961, twelve grandchildren were born, five boys and seven girls. It was the Era of the Babies: Someone was always pregnant, lying around the pool liked a beached whale in a maternity bathing suit.

Ranny, Angus' brother, and his wife, Helen, had three: a daughter Dinny and two sons, Mark and Archie. Sally, his sister, who had given the party where Angus and I met, and her husband, Taf, had four: three daughters, Maggy, Sara and Susannah, and a son, Evan; and we had five: Sandy, Kate, Jim, Betsy and Anne. Of the twelve grandchildren, eight grew up on the Place.

In 1956 Angus' sister, Sally, left. Her husband had had a bellyful of communal living and wanted to strike out on his own. Moving progressively westward across the country, she and her family eventually put down permanent roots in Santa Barbara, California. But every summer she brought the children back to visit.

After she left, the red cottage on the road was vacant. Mac's bachelor cousin Aden, a New York cardiologist with an apartment on the Upper East Side, decided to rent it for a weekend retreat and used it for the rest of his life.

Between 1952 and 1956 though, the three McIntyre siblings were all living on the farm with their respective families, and in 1953, I had only one baby to deal with, not five. A redheaded insomniac, Sandy was proving to be a twenty-four hour job.

From the start there was never any question about who was in charge. He cried, I ran. He burped, I jumped. He threw up, I panicked. I was finding out in a hurry that a fashion job in the city was no preparation for changing diapers, sterilizing bottles or excelling at motherhood. Babies were even more of a mystery than hemlines.

In addition, my new modern house had all the charm of a Jersey City warehouse. Not a single rug, curtain or decorative touch was anywhere to be seen. In the living room sat a worn white leather couch we had bought secondhand, a blond wood coffee table that had been a wedding present, and a chair the color of coffee with cream. For light, there were overhead recessed spots, one standing lamp and an ugly space-age table lamp bought at a country yard sale.

"Now when are you going to do something about this house, Bobbie?" Margaret had stopped by to see the baby and have afternoon tea. Houses were very important to Margaret.

"I haven't gotten around to it," I bridled. "The baby takes all my time."

"It needs some color," Margaret went on, surveying the room. "You have almost no color at all. Like that chair," she said, eyeing my one upholstered chair.

"That's café au lait," I said. "It's a lovely color, it goes with everything."

"Oh is that what it is?" she laughed. "In Benton we called that you-know-what brown."

No I didn't know what, but remembering my conversation with Louise, I had a pretty good idea. Mercifully the baby cried and we changed the subject.

Outside, things were no better. Instead of the instant carpeting of bright green sod and flowering fruit trees that grace the houses in magazines, our new house was surrounded by a sea of mud.

I didn't know where to begin.

By day I was reading Dr. Spock and Gesell, at night I was devouring House and Garden and Living for Young Homemakers. But no matter how incompetent I felt, I wouldn't have dreamed of asking Margaret for advice. I just assumed she knew even less than I did.

At first I kept to myself, totally preoccupied with the baby and the house. In the mornings I made formula and did laundry, and in the afternoons I took Sandy on a walk to the back fields where Mac kept the pigs. But, finally, one day, shortly after I'd bought a sisal rug and hung some burlap curtains that were making me sneeze, I screwed up my courage and invited the family to dinner.

I served a precooked ham, which I forgot to warm in the oven; some baked potatoes, which were undercooked; iceberg lettuce with some dressing out of a bottle, French bread and wine. Since I had no dining room table, we ate on our laps.

After dinner I carried all the dishes back into the kitchen and loaded them in the dishwasher.

"What's that?" said Sally, frowning at the machine installed neatly to the left of the sink.

"A dishwasher," I said. "Isn't it great? See, you rinse the dishes and load them in, add soap, close and press this button. The machine washes, rinses and dries them all." I beamed with how wonderful it all was.

Sally eyed it skeptically, as I started loading.

"Well, it seems to me," she said, "that if you have to go to all the trouble of rinsing and scrubbing the dishes before you put them in, you might as well go all the way and wash them too."

She turned around to bring more dishes over and continued to watch.

"I really can't see that it saves you any trouble or time," she concluded.

"I've never thought that washing dishes was such a big deal," said Helen, Ranny's wife. "I can't imagine ever wanting one."

Margaret wandered into the kitchen to see what was going on and quickly decided she wasn't interested. She never did dishes anyway, except when the help was off, so a dishwasher was definitely not high on her list of priorities.

"What's for dessert?" she said, moving on to more important things. "You can't have a dinner party without dessert."

Three weeks later all the houses on the Place had installed Kitchenaid dishwashers and I had jump-started the family into the technological age. My new modern kitchen was a pacesetter, all right, but the stuff coming out of it was another story.

All that, however, was about to change. Bad food, I was soon to learn, was the cardinal sin, and the Polar Club ice cream I had served Margaret for dessert that night, beneath contempt.

PART TWO

Food

ONE

Newt Gingrich didn't know what he was talking about that night in '95 when he lectured the country on family values. Again and again he called our attention to orphanages, The Saturday Evening Post and the Boy Scout handbook, when Margaret could have told him in a minute that family values were nothing of the sort.

Family values were about food, pure and simple. About buying it, about cooking it (not that she ever did) and most of all about eating it. Food, to Margaret, was the way you showed love; nothing else even came close.

Any fool knew that an orphanage was the last place on earth to get a good meal.

TWO

Margaret cared about three things, not necessarily in any order. She cared about family, she cared about food and she cared about how things looked. Especially herself. But if I had to pick the absolute love of her life, it would be food. Welcome to Benton country where food is king.

Not long after I had moved onto the Place, Margaret and I had the following conversation.

"I wish," said Margaret, breathing into the telephone, "that you could remember what you had to eat."

Eight-fifteen on a Sunday morning is not when I'm thinking about food. I hadn't gotten to bed until after midnight the night before and only an hour later I was up again feeding the baby.

"It was just a cocktail party," I yawned. "People were drinking, not eating."

"Yes, but you must have had *something* to eat," she persisted.

I racked my brain trying to think whether or not I'd had something to eat.

It had been our first social outing since Sandy's birth and I could hardly wait to get out of the house and see someone my own age. I had barely been able to zip up a little pre-pregnancy number, since I still had a good ten pounds to lose, and food was the last thing on my mind.

"I suppose there were some potato chips, dips, you know, stuff like that. You could just help yourself. I don't think anybody passed anything to me, if that's what you mean."

I could have told her who was there, what they were wearing, who had too much to drink and who was coming on to who's wife. But *eat*?

Margaret sighed deeply at the other end of the phone. This was not going to be a satisfying conversation. When it came to discussions of food, I soon learned, Margaret liked chapter and verse.

"It doesn't sound like a very good party," she concluded and changed the subject. "What did you wear?"

THREE

Growing up, I had paid almost no attention to food. People ate because they had to, but it was nothing to get excited about. My family had a cook, and our house was known for its good food; but my family was more concerned with whether we had our elbows on the table or our fingernails were clean, than whether the roast was properly cooked. Along with money, my parents did not consider food a proper topic of conversation.

When Margaret came into my life, all that changed.

My own cooking career got off to an unpromising start soon after my marriage. I had just returned from our honeymoon with the sinking feeling that I was going to have to learn to cook. I thought cooking was something that other people did.

The subject of cooking and who was going to do it had first come up on Cape Cod. Angus and I had rented a house on the beach there following our wedding, and like most houses this one came with a kitchen. After determining that I was indeed a stranger to the stove, Angus, in a burst of enlightened self-interest (or perhaps envisioning a dreary future of canned Spam and Franco-American spaghetti), announced he would teach me how to fry an egg.

"Here's what you do," he said brightly one morning, using the same encouraging tone of voice you would use to explain toilet training to a recalcitrant three-year-old.

"First you cook the bacon in the frying pan. Then, leaving some fat in the pan, you carefully break the egg into the fat."

"Then," he went on, "after it sets for a minute or two, you tip the pan ever so slightly and start spooning hot fat over the top of the egg. As you baste it, the top gradually turns white and when it's all white the egg is done! This way the yolk cooks without having to turn it over and break it."

Angus is very good at explaining things. Having cooked a perfect fried egg, he retired from cooking and it was months before I realized that a fried egg was the only dish in his repertoire. If his mother had ever demonstrated anything else, he must have been out of the room.

Anyway, here I was back in our New York apartment and, as they say, the honeymoon was over. I could boil water and fry an egg, but what did I do for an encore? Even my post-college year of living in my mother's New York duplex had done nothing for my cooking skills. I either ate out or alternated between hamburgers and chicken pot pies if she wasn't around to cook.

There was nothing for it but to go out and buy a cookbook, the biggest one I could find.

The one I bought, "The Joy of Cooking", I raced through in a single day, all 834 pages of it. By evening I was so fired up Angus thought I must be reading "Lady Chatterley's Lover". After plowing through what seemed like more than 5,000 recipes, I had become an instant expert. I was now qualified to invite a guest to dinner and invite one I did, even though as yet nothing worth mentioning had emerged from my kitchen. It was not one of my better ideas.

My menu, I decided, would be cheese fondue, a nostalgic reminder of an academic year I had spent in Switzerland. Besides, the man I had invited to be my first guest had become my friend in Geneva.

Cheese fondue is, of course, a Swiss national passion. Everyone sits around a table guzzling wine and poking chunks of French bread, which are impaled on the ends of long forks, into a pot of bubbling cheese. What really caught my eye, though, when I read the recipe, was that fondue had only four ingredients, a level of complication that even I could manage.

The recipe stated that all I had to do was rub an earthenware casserole with garlic, add dry white wine and grated Swiss cheese, turn on the gas and stir. Then, just before serving, throw in a splash of kirsch. How could I miss!

It was a meal to remember. My fondue separated and my pot separated. What my new cookbook hadn't bothered to mention was that unless you add about a teaspoon of cornstarch dissolved in the kirsch at the end, that fondue isn't *ever* going to get it together.

While I stirred and stirred and the fondue boiled and boiled, Angus and the old friend drank and drank in the living room. When I heard the cork popping out of the third bottle of wine, I decided we had better eat. Who cares whether or not a fondue is perfectly smooth?

I carefully lifted the bubbling pot off the burner. But, alas, my new cookbook had also neglected to mention that you cannot put an earthenware casserole on a gas burner and turn it on full blast. The bottom of the pot having cracked neatly all around the bottom edge, stayed snugly on the burner; and the fondue, thus set free, began to ooze slowly off the stove and onto the floor.

When I had finally quieted down, Angus brought the basket of cut-up French bread and the remaining wine back into the kitchen; and we all sat on the floor and ate dinner. I reassured everyone through my tears that the floor was perfectly clean, but I needn't have bothered. After three bottles of wine, they couldn't have cared less.

After the fiasco over the fondue, it was back to frozen chicken pot pies and hamburgers. And it wasn't until we moved to the country, with Margaret next door, that my food education began in earnest. From a lifetime of barely noticing what I had to eat, I quickly learned to pay attention to everything.

Margaret was a woman so enamored of the whole subject of food that she perceived her life primarily as a series of culinary flashbacks. She looked back on her childhood, an unforgettable succession of cakes, pies, hot rolls and pork roasts, with all the passionate yearning of a woman looking back on her first love. While the rest of us fantasized about sex and money, Margaret dreamt of peach cobblers and lemon meringue pies.

"Oh," Margaret would moan, her eyes closed in ecstasy, "our house had the most delicious food. You never tasted anything like it. And Mama always had plenty, in case someone dropped by at the last moment. And the desserts! You've never *seen* such desserts. Every night." Talking about food, it seemed, was almost as rewarding as eating it.

I soon got in the habit of calling her after I'd been to a dinner party and giving her a detailed description of everything I had to eat. We would then have a riveting conversation concerning everything on the menu.

Margaret always wanted to know, too, who had actually cooked the meal and whether there had been any help. Discussing help, particularly her own, was also endlessly compelling. Some could cook food properly, some could not. Most fell woefully short of cooking the food of her dreams.

As far as I know, Margaret never cooked anything. That's what the help were for. Though she knew exactly how something should taste and look, she didn't really have any interest in doing it. Margaret had one rule and one rule only about food: it had to taste good. Nutritional ramifications never entered her head.

"Most people," she sniffed, "don't know what good food tastes like."

FOUR

Benton, Illinois, is technically above the Mason-Dixon line, but its heart and soul is in the south. The food that Mac and Margaret loved was the food they'd been raised on, down home Southern cooking at its greasiest best. Nutritionally, the diet was an unmitigated disaster, a precursor of every killer disease of the 20th century. But as the comedian Redd Foxx once exclaimed, there's no point in lying around a hospital dying of nothing. It was worth every bite.

The cooks who worked in Margaret's kitchen after she first moved to the country were long on temperament and short on talent. There was ill-tempered Agnes, who thought quantity was an adequate substitute for quality; and crazy Dora, whose cooking tended to mirror her manic cycles. During her high phase, she preferred to wash cars; and during her low phase, she made lemon chicken five days a week.

The cooks came and went with depressing regularity, but it wasn't until William and Janie Grant arrived from Aiken, South Carolina, that the cooking began to resemble the stuff of Margaret's dreams.

William and Janie cooked Southern, and Southern cooking meant food cooked long and slow. In Margaret's book, there was no such thing as meat that was cooked too long. A rare leg of lamb to her was simply underdone; she wanted hers roasted until it fell off the bone. A rare roast beef she didn't consider fit to serve. As for nouvelle vegetables, they might as well have been left raw, for all she enjoyed them. She wanted hers cooked soft and mushy, preferably with a nice piece of salt pork thrown in for flavor.

As often as not, William and Janie fried the food, either in butter, bacon grease or lard. Meat was never served without gravy, homemade hotbreads always came with plenty of butter. Nobody worried about fat grams; nobody knew what a fat gram was. Fat was what made food taste good, everyone knew that. How can you make proper fried chicken if you take away the skin?

Margaret's kitchen marched on fried chicken. The help ate it almost every day; Margaret would have too if she hadn't always been trying to diet. It wasn't so much that she was on a strict diet; she just tried to limit herself, so she could overindulge in the food she loved.

"You would not believe what they're eating for lunch in there," she groaned. We were sitting talking on her porch, where she was having her usual diet lunch of lowfat cottage cheese and two pieces of Swedish blotting paper, as Mac called her Wasa bread. "They" referred to William and Janie, and Louetta, who came during the week to clean.

"Here I am, starved half to death, trying to get down to human size, and they're having fried chicken and rice and homemade biscuits.

Of course they're all so fat they can hardly get around." She looked miserable. "I'd give anything to have some."

William cooked chicken instinctively; he couldn't remember a time when he hadn't known how to do it.

First he cut up a fryer and soaked it in milk. Next he sprinkled the pieces with salt and pepper and dredged them in flour. At this point, he let the chicken rest while he did other things.

Then he took a large iron skillet, filled it with about two inches of melted bacon grease and butter, turned the gas on to medium high and started frying. He kept turning the chicken pieces over and over, starting with the dark meat, which took longer to cook. Eventually when all the pieces were a beautiful crispy golden brown, he would remove them to some paper toweling and keep them warm while he made cream gravy.

He always served the chicken with Carolina rice that was cooked with a tablespoon of bacon grease added to the boiling water, and hot homemade biscuits slathered with butter.

A Southern fried chicken dinner was a feast for the gods. No poached chicken cutlet ever came close.

But even a fried chicken dinner, as far as Margaret was concerned, was only a preamble to the main point of any meal: dessert. She had a sweet tooth that would have shamed a five-year-old.

Her preferred way of eating was to hold back on the dinner so she could have at least two portions of dessert. And at the top of her list of preferred desserts were pies and puddings.

The litmus test of a new cook was whether or not she could make a lemon meringue pie. Or a creme brulée. Janie could make both, but her specialty was soufflé: hot chocolate soufflé served with cold whipped cream, and vanilla soufflé served with a hot grand marnier sauce. But nothing inspired the orgy of rapture that a fresh peach cobbler brought on: For Margaret it was the Hope Diamond of all desserts, especially when served with homemade vanilla ice cream.

FIVE

As Margaret and I got to know each other, my interest in cooking began to pick up. Anyone who could get off on a lemon meringue pie, I reasoned, must know something I didn't. Memories of the disastrous fondue began to recede, and the idea that even I could learn to cook began to seem, if not probable, at least possible. I decided to buy three more cookbooks and gear up. I would begin by experimenting on my family.

"No," my son said at mealtime to almost everything he was offered. "No," he'd repeat, shaking his head and dropping the offending food on the floor with the precision of a B-1 bomber pilot.

Not to worry, Dr. Spock wrote soothingly. "Children have a remarkable inborn mechanism that lets them know how much food and which type of food they need for normal growth and development. Make mealtime pleasant." In other words, a classic picky eater will outgrow it, and in the meantime, just give him what he wants.

But when weeks went by with nothing but hamburger and ice cream crossing his lips, I concluded that experimenting on Sandy was out of the question. That left Angus and Margaret.

Angus cheerfully ate whatever was put in front of him, happy he didn't have to fix it himself. Margaret was more discerning. "I think those cookies need more vanilla," she said, the first time I made chocolate chip cookies and invited her to tea. "But they're still good," she reassured me, wolfing down six in rapid succession.

The next time I made them I added more vanilla, and just like she said, they were better.

Pretty soon I grew more confident, even hazarding a small dinner party now and then. And when no one complained or came down with food poisoning, I at last felt ready to tackle something big.

Margaret's birthday was coming up in a couple of weeks and I thought it would be fun to throw a surprise luncheon for her and invite all her friends. It would be a perfect opportunity to show off my newly acquired culinary skills, and who knows, I might even make a lemon meringue pie.

But as I went about making up the guest list with the help of Mac, I soon discovered that Margaret's "friends" were not "friends" in the usual sense; they were all related. They consisted of a large network of family members with whom she was constantly in touch. There were first cousins, second cousins, cousins once removed, cousins by marriage and even kissing cousins. Almost all originally came from Benton and were now scattered over the New York area.

Socializing with family members was a whole new concept to me. My mother had seldom seen her only brother, and if she enjoyed the company of my father's relatives that was news to me.

On a cold, bright March 17, a birthday Margaret shared with St. Patrick, I met her extended kin group for the first time.

Tusie

ONE

Of all the extended kin group I invited to Margaret's birthday party on that sunny March day, none loomed larger in her life than her cousin Tusie. Had Tusie not existed, Margaret would have had to invent her: word for word, Tusie provided more conversational fodder than any other single subject.

There was nothing the two women didn't discuss at least once, sometimes twice or more a day. Food was the topic of choice.

"I'm too fat," Tusie would say on the telephone. It was her standard opening greeting.

"Well, my stomach is sticking out a mile," Margaret would counter on the other end.

"What are you having for dinner tonight?" Tusie would ask, and the conversation was off and running, a never-ending litany of menus, recipes, cooking tips and dieting lore.

Tusie was Margaret's first cousin, but she was no ordinary cousin. The two women were as close and competitive as sisters. Actually they might as well have been sisters. Tusie, the youngest in a family of four siblings, moved in with Margaret's family at the age of eight when her mother ran off with a violinist; and there she stayed until the day she married.

To no ones surprise, Tusie married early, a young man named George Boone whom she'd met at the University of Illinois summer school. What Tusie craved after the turmoil of her childhood was the normalcy of her own home and her own family. No other career choice looked remotely appealing.

Eventually, she and George left Illinois; and after brief interludes in Indiana and New York City, they settled permanently in Douglaston, Long Island, where they raised their only child, George Jr. But it wasn't until Margaret herself was married almost forty years later, and also living on Long Island, that their lives came together once more.

I met Tusie and the rest of the kin group for the first time the day of my surprise party for Margaret.

The guest list was as follows:

There was Muriel, of the "hound-dog" face, whose picture had so outraged Elizabeth Arden. Though Muriel wasn't strictly family, she felt like family. She and Margaret had shared a life on the stage and a life after the stage, and continued to stay in touch. Muriel was now happily married to a portly Englishman named Theo. Unlike her first wealthy sportsman husband, Theo had little money and no visible means of support; but he had a kind and loving disposition, and shared with Muriel a vast appetite for food and drink.

My old nemesis Louise, who was also Margaret's cousin, was by this time widowed and living in New York City. Her son Bill, my erstwhile boyfriend, had married a thoroughly suitable young woman with impeccable credentials; and Louise, her job done, had left St. Louis and moved east. In New York she surrounded herself with a lively group of amusing and attentive young men, playing cards and going to the theater. The day of my party she hired a limousine to bring her to the country.

To my amazement, she was all sweetness and light that day, bringing me two flowering pink azaleas for my living room and raving about how good everything tasted. She seemed to have completely forgotten that my English had ever offended her.

Second cousin Ruth was always referred to in the family as "poor old Ruth." She was an elderly spinster whose bladder, Margaret said, was set too close to her eyes. Life's vagaries affected her so deeply that she could hardly string three sentences together without her eyes brimming over with tears.

Vivian and Ralph Swain were also Long Island transplants. Vivian was Tusie's older sister, but there the resemblance ended. Forced to work almost all her life, she was stern and no-nonsense.

It was Vivian who had raised her two younger brothers when her mother left home with the violinist; and Vivian who, as a young bride in St. Louis, had started Jeanne Vivian's Tea Room Restaurant to flesh out her husband's small income.

The Tea Room had been a hit from the start. One of the black cooks had brought with him a sinfully rich dessert called Fudge Pie, which had put the restaurant on the map. The hand-printed menu, rich in Bentonese, always listed Fudge Pie (which was served with vanilla ice cream) as coming "with a la mode upon it."

Now many years later and living on Long Island, Vivian gave piano lessons to small children in the afternoon and in the morning she ran a playgroup for three-and four-year-olds. Viv's husband, Ralph, who had been a violinist with the St. Louis Symphony (an irony not lost on the rest of the family) was now in the early stages of dementia; but even before he got sick, earning a living had never been his strong suit.

Another guest, Chris, a thin energetic woman whose daughter had married one of the Swain boys, had moved east to be near her daughter when her own marriage failed.

And lastly there was Aden, Mac's cousin Aden, who also came from Benton, just like everyone else. Aden was a well-known New York cardiologist, widely respected in his field, but as far as Margaret was concerned he was just another lost soul. He lived by himself on the Upper East Side in a big gloomy apartment hung with red velvet curtains and heavy Moroccan tapestries. His life was programmed by a bossy Swedish cook named Elsa and two nasty terriers named Jenny and Captain.

But most importantly for Margaret, there was Tusie. Tusie and her husband, George. George was running a successful refrigeration business on the East Coast which now included his son; and Tusie lived the life of an affluent suburban Long Island housewife, playing bridge, talking on the telephone and eating too much.

I had asked all my luncheon guests to arrive at noon sharp the day of the party and they happily obliged. At 12:30 Mac drove up with

Margaret. She must have known that something was up because her hair had been freshly done and she was wearing a beautiful new suit. As she walked into my living room to the cries of "Happy Birthday!" her face lit up in the most enormous smile. She looked around at all her family and started to jump up and down and clap her hands. "Isn't this *wonderful*!" she cried, "all the people I *love*! Oh, this is so exciting, it's a sight on earth!"

"Yes," answered Tusie, giving her a kiss, "it's most definitely a sight on earth."

I had changed my menu at least ten times, trying to come up with the perfect lunch, and had finally opted for something that didn't need heating at the last minute. Though I was counting on my son, Sandy, being down for his nap when we ate, naps were never a sure thing.

I needn't have worried. The party was one of the few times that Margaret barely noticed what she had to eat. I had made a delicious chef salad with the dressing made from scratch, hot biscuits and three kinds of desserts. But she was so busy laughing and talking and being the life of the party, that she hardly had time to put anything into her mouth.

That night when Angus got home from work he asked Sandy if the birthday party had been fun.

"Yep," said Sandy, pushing a train across the living room rug, "it was a sight on earth."

TWO

Sometimes, when I think back on all the good folk from Benton, I think there must have been something in the town water that caused such an obsession with food, since clearly everyone seemed to suffer from the same affliction. But this didn't really occur to me until after I'd heard the story of Tusie and the fudge:

It was late afternoon, toward the end of February, and the weather couldn't have been more miserable. Outside a mixture of rain and snow pelted the frozen ground, and on top of the curved roof of her small greenhouse Tusie noticed that at least two inches of frozen slush had already fallen.

It had been a good day not to go anywhere, she thought, a good day to stay home. She wandered into her kitchen, wondering what to do with herself, half glad she didn't have to cook dinner tonight, yet still wanting a little treat, when it struck her that the one thing in this world she would adore to have was fudge. Beautiful, dark, rich, glistening chocolate fudge. She could practically taste it.

Wasn't it lucky, she thought, that her husband, George, was in Chicago on a business trip. George wasn't too crazy about her making fudge. Actually what George really didn't like was her eating fudge. Tusie knew that he thought she was too fat, but at moments like this, she was able to push such irritating ideas right out of her mind.

She didn't even have to look up the recipe; she knew it by heart. She knew it in her sleep. And as luck would have it, all the ingredients she needed were right there in her kitchen. She pulled the bitter chocolate off the shelf of her food closet, scooped a cup of sugar out of the jar on the counter and yanked a stick of butter out of the fridge. She could hardly wait.

Thirty minutes later as darkness fell, the whole house smelled of chocolate and the fudge was done. Tusie took it out of the oven and put it down on the kitchen counter to cool. She knew it should sit for at least an hour in order to be cut properly into squares; but the pungent smell of warm chocolate was so overwhelming that waiting was out of the question.

With the quick decisiveness of a cat ambushing a mouse, she threw the fudge in the freezer and went into the living room to lock the front door. She then pulled down all the shades, turned off the lights and switched on the television set. What fun, she thought, as the television warmed up: Older women were being interviewed who had had affairs with much younger men.

She raced back to the freezer and grabbed the fudge, snatched a serving spoon out of the silver chest, and flew back into the living room. She didn't want to miss a thing. As she sank back into the soft chintz sofa, the pot holder and pan of hot fudge in one hand, a large silver spoon in the other, Tusie breathed a sigh of total contentment.

One of the women on the show was now being asked how she had managed to keep her son from finding out that she was having an affair with his best friend. Where did she and her lover have their rendezvous anyway? This was really getting interesting, Tusie thought, as she glanced down and discovered she had already eaten half the pan.

Just as the second woman started to tell where she had first met her lover, the doorbell rang. It's probably one of the neighbors, Tusie thought, and stealthily reached forward to turn the volume down to a whisper. Maybe they'll think nobody's home and go away.

All was quiet, but pretty soon the doorbell rang again, along with a pounding on the front door. Tusie didn't move a muscle. Any fool would know there's no one home, she thought; all the lights are off.

Woman number three was now being interviewed, a grey-haired grandmother of two who wasn't exactly your everyday sex object. Tusie was hypnotized. She could really relate to this woman in her neat navy blue suit and her wavy grey hair. She especially loved the suit. Margaret said Tusie always bought the same thing when she went clothes shopping and she supposed that was somewhat true. Just last week she had counted nine navy blue suits in her closet, but of course navy was very becoming. It matched her eyes.

Tusie stared hard at the grandmother wondering if maybe she had missed something in life, never having had an affair. She didn't really think that any of the people she knew had had affairs, and anyway she couldn't imagine going to bed with any other man but George, her husband of almost forty years. One thing was certain though. If she ever did have an affair, she'd definitely have to do something about her stomach.

The pounding on the door started in earnest now, accompanied by some thunderous kicks.

Tusie sighed deeply and turned off the television set; and concealing the pan of half-eaten fudge behind her back, cautiously opened the door and peered out. The angry red face of her longtime husband glared back at her in the dark.

"What the HELL is going on around here anyway?" boomed George, pushing past Tusie into the pitch black living room.

"Why George Boone," she sputtered, "you aren't supposed to be home until tomorrow night!"

THREE

Funny, talkative and terminally nosy, Tusie was first and foremost a social animal. Not ever, in His wildest plan, did God intend her to live alone. So when George, her 67-year-old husband walked off the golf course one day in 1958 while vacationing in Pompano Beach and dropped dead of a major heart attack, Tusie was beyond consolation. At 62 she considered herself much too young to be a widow and most certainly too young to live alone.

For the longest time Tusie could hardly summon the energy to get up in the morning or go to bed at night. She'd call Margaret on the phone and then she'd called Louise. She'd called her sister Vivian, who was too busy, and then her daughter-in-law, who was even busier. Nothing helped. "I'm so lonesome I could die," she told anyone who would listen.

And then one day, after a couple of years had gone by, Louise called and had the bright idea that she and Tusie should do a grand tour of Europe. It was time, she said, that Tusie got out of the house, bought some new clothes, got her hair styled and stopped moping around. Louise knew just the countries they should visit and how to plan the whole trip. What's more, her wealthy friend, Elsie, a jolly widow who was currently tipping the scales at 300 pounds, was eager to join them.

It was just the catalyst that Tusie needed.

The three sixtyish widows, it was decided, would all sail to France. None of them liked to fly and five days on shipboard sounded like a pleasantly relaxing way to begin a journey.

The voyage across was everything they'd hoped for. The seas were calm, the other passengers congenial, the food bountiful. Louise had a moment's panic wondering if she would be seated at the Captain's table, but as it turned out she needn't have worried. Ship captains know all about the needs of single ladies travelling alone. It's part of their job description, like knowing how to dance.

All three ladies spent several festive evenings dining at the head table, each one certain that Captain Elstrom had eyes only for her. Louise would have liked to have been singled out for special consideration, but in the end she conceded that it probably was nice they were all included.

Five days later the ship chugged into Cherbourg, where the ladies were met by a volatile Frenchman named Emilio driving a very large Mercedes. Keeping up a steady stream of French and English invective, Emilio laboriously piled their mountain of luggage into the back of his limousine (Louise had insisted on a limousine), and then politely assisting each lady into the car, proceeded to drive them on their tour of the continent.

For six delightful weeks they toured France, Switzerland, Germany, Italy and Austria, staying in charming hotels and country inns (Louise had insisted on consulting the Relais et Chateaux guide whenever possible), dressing up for the theater and the opera (Elsie, who was hard of hearing, had managed to get excellent seats through her many connections), taking V.I.P. tours through famous museums (Elsie's connections again) and sampling with huge gusto the local cuisines and wines.

When they arrived in Vienna towards the end of their tour, Elsie picked up the phone in her room at the Imperial Hotel and called the American ambassador. He was an old friend whom she had known all her life; and when he heard she was going to be in Vienna with her two friends for a week or more, he insisted on throwing a welcoming cocktail party the following night.

The next evening the ladies, resplendent in shimmering brocade and sparkling jewels, swept into the ambassadorial residence, three ships in full sail. Tusie had gained at least ten pounds since the start of the trip, but it didn't bother her in the least. Since she was weighing herself in kilos now (one kilo equals 2.2 pounds), ten pounds seemed like a drop in the bucket.

The lovely Old World drawing room of the embassy, softly lit with crystal chandeliers, was already buzzing with the happy murmur of guests when they arrived. The ambassador had invited not only a large representation of the American community currently living in Vienna, but also a judicious sprinkling of interesting Austrians.

Tusie, who drank only sparingly, decided to jump-start herself with a scotch and soda. Except for Elsie and Louise she didn't know a soul in this room.

"Good evening," said a grey-haired gentleman walking up to Tusie and giving her a slight bow. He was wearing a black Bavarian jacket with unusual wooden buttons and he had a decidedly foreign accent.

"That's a most ravishing dress you're wearing. It just matches your eyes." He smiled and pulled a cigarette out of his breast pocket. "My name by the way is Arthur. I wanted to welcome you to Vienna." He paused briefly to light his cigarette with a monogrammed silver lighter. "I noticed you the moment you came in," he added.

Tusie felt her color rise. She wondered who in the world this man was who was staring at her so intently and telling her how attractive she was. She wished now she hadn't gained those ten pounds. She reached up and smoothed her hair and smiled flirtatiously back. Maybe it was the dress, maybe it was just the scotch. Whatever it was, she hadn't had this much fun in years.

Arthur had arrived at the party early. He had heard the party was in honor of three American widows travelling abroad and had thought it prudent to be punctual. Stationing himself by the bar, the best vantage point, he had watched the three ladies enter the room. In no time at all he had concluded that Tusie looked like the best bet.

During the evening he scarcely left her side. He let drop that he was a member of the Austrian aristocracy, that he was a widower and that he spoke eleven languages. "I would be honored to show you and your friends Vienna," he said, "since you are going to be here for a week. There is much to see." He smiled encouragingly. "I will call you at your hotel in the morning," he said at the end of the evening, as he leaned over to kiss her hand.

"You wouldn't believe it; we're being shown around Vienna by an Austrian count," burbled Tusie, during an excited call home to Margaret a few days later. "He's the most fascinating man, so cultured, and knows the city like the back of his hand. And you should see the wonderful little restaurants he's taking us to for lunch and dinner. They're divine! And you know, he's absolutely crazy about *me*! I can tell."

"Who's paying for all the lunches and the dinners?" said Margaret.

"Well," said Tusie, "we are, of course. We have to do something to pay him back for all the time he's spending on us. He won't let us pay him a thing."

There was silence on the other end. Then, "He's more likely some no-count," said Margaret. "You'd better be careful."

"Why are you always so suspicious?" said Tusie. "He really is crazy about me. He says I'm so much more attractive than Elsie and Louise."

"Well that wouldn't be much of a trick," chortled Margaret on the other end.

The warm summer days sped by in a rosy haze of round-the-clock sightseeing and marathon meals; and at the end of the week Arthur took Tusie out for dinner alone to a romantic candlelit bistro and asked her to marry him. He said he had never met a woman so beautiful and charming. Tusie's glasses were so steamed up she could barely see across the table, but she beamed with pleasure and reached for his hand.

The next day she called her son on Long Island and said she was getting married.

FOUR

"Well for God's sake," said Margaret. "Now I've heard everything. Why she's only known him for a week. Clearly she's lost her mind."

Tusie's son, George, had called to break the news.

"You don't think she's serious do you?"

"I'm afraid she is," said George. "She wants Anne and me and the Woods to fly over for the wedding next week."

"Jesus Christ on a rail," said Margaret, exhaling loudly into the phone.

The Woods were Betty Wood, an old, old friend who was now a widow, and Betty's son, Bob, and his wife, Beverly.

"So I guess we're going to go. Mother says she needs some family support and needs us to come immediately. She says we're going to love Arthur."

"Yes, I know you will," cackled Margaret on the other end.

Three days later George and his wife, Anne, flew with the Woods to Vienna and checked into the Imperial Hotel. And once more, the American ambassador gathered the community together for a combination welcoming and pre-wedding celebration.

At the height of the party the following evening, with champagne corks popping and toasts being made, Tusie went up to her son and said she had to speak to him privately. Right away. Her eyes were filled with tears.

"I'm afraid I've made the most terrible mistake," she said, starting to cry. "I don't think I can go through with it."

"Then don't," said George. "It's all right. Nobody will be mad at you."

George put his arms around his mother to comfort her and felt her tension slowly begin to ease.

"Elsie and Louise talked me into it," she sniffed, blowing her nose and wiping her eyes. "They were all for it."

Seeing Arthur alongside George and his wife, Anne, had instantly brought home to Tusie their contrasting worlds. Never would he have anything in common with either her family or her friends, and the sooner she admitted this, the better.

In order to let Arthur down as gently as possible, the decision was made to "delay" the wedding. The Woods and the young Boones, ever resilient, said that as long as they were in Europe they might as well see some of it and asked Arthur for his advice. They had learned that Arthur was not really a count, as advertised; he was a tour director, which probably explained how he knew so much about the surrounding area and was fluent in so many languages.

Everyone opted to go in a different direction and agreed to meet in Paris a week later. The young Boones took off for the Riviera, the Woods preferred to see Austria and Arthur joined the three ladies to do a leisurely trip through Provence. He still hoped that Tusie might be persuaded to marry him.

In Paris they all had a festive reunion with two days at the Ritz, dinner at Maxim's and a night at the Crazy Horse Saloon. And then it was time to say goodbye to Arthur.

As he left he said to Tusie that perhaps he would come to the States one day and see her again. "Perhaps," she said, smiling and waving him on.

"I really don't understand why he wanted to marry me," she said after he'd gone. "We didn't have that much in common."

"Arthur's what's known as a fortune hunter," George said gently. "He thought you were a wealthy widow."

"But I don't have a fortune", said Tusie.

"That's right, but he didn't know that," George said. "He probably got you mixed up with Barbara Hutton."

FIVE

After more than six weeks on the road Louise and Elsie concluded they had had enough of Europe. They were tired of sleeping in strange lumpy beds and eating food that gave them indigestion. As soon as they could arrange it, they were on a plane back home.

Tusie, meanwhile, flush with a renewed zest for living and relieved to be rid of Arthur, went on to England for a short visit by herself. She had never been to England before; and now that she was this close, it seemed a shame not to go. Besides, she had heard that Charles Thompson's wife had died and she thought she might look him up. The Thompsons were English friends of Muriel and Theo, whom Tusie had met on several of their visits to Long Island, but she hadn't seen Charles in ages.

In London, Tusie booked a room at the Dorchester. As soon as she had unpacked her bag and hung up all her clothes, she went downstairs to the beauty salon and had her hair done. She then bought a magazine to read in her room and a packet of safety pins in case she had trouble zipping up the skirt of her favorite blue suit.

Around 3:30 she ordered tea and biscuits sent up to her room; and after finishing her tea, she took a long leisurely bath. By this time it was 4:30 and she couldn't think of another thing to do. She took a very deep breath, picked up the phone and called Charles Thompson.

From the tone of his voice she wasn't a hundred percent sure he knew exactly who she was, but he cheerfully agreed to meet her that evening at the Dorchester. He suggested that they have a drink at the hotel and renew old acquaintances; and then, since she had never been to London before, go somewhere else for dinner. He would make the dinner reservation and meet her in the lobby around 6:00.

Tusie was ecstatic. She tried on everything she had brought with her, decided they were all wrong and tried them all on again.

Finally she decided on the very first thing she'd put on, her becoming navy blue suit with the white silk blouse and her Hermes scarf with the pink roses. Everyone always told her how rested she looked when she had it on.

Tusie looked at her watch. It still was only twenty to six; but she was getting so fidgety sitting in her room, she decided to go down and sit in the lobby. People-watching would distract her.

On the dot of 6:00, an impeccably dressed grey-haired gentleman sporting a mustache and carrying a walking cane, came striding through the front entrance. Once in the lobby he stopped and looked carefully around. It was obvious he had come to meet somebody.

Jumping to her feet and walking toward him with her hands outstretched and a wide smile on her expectant face, Tusie said, "Why Charles Thompson, I would have known you anywhere!"

It wasn't Charles at all.

Chastened, Tusie sat down and after a few moments Charles himself walked in the door. He went straight up to Tusie without a moment's hesitation and gave her a welcoming kiss.

"My deah," he said, "how perfectly lovely to see you again," and Tusie's eyes misted over with pleasure.

When she left London a week later, Tusie invited Charles to visit her on Long Island. "You have a lot of friends there" she urged, "who would all love to see you again. And so would I."

Charles came; and after several more trips he and Tusie decided to marry. Tusie was 67. It had been five years since George had died and time to move on. And for Charles, 69, widowed and retired, it was also time to move on.

The wedding was held in New York City at the Fifth Avenue Presbyterian Church with a reception immediately following at the St. Regis. The entire family was delighted. Even Margaret said that Charles Thompson was the nicest man she'd ever met.

For the rest of their lives Tusie and Charles divided their time between Hampshire, England, and Long Island. Charles had two married daughters living in England and seven grandchildren, and Tusie had her son and his wife living in St. James on Long Island with six grandchildren.

Though she became thoroughly immersed in British life, discovering the joys of trifle and lemon curd and obsessing endlessly about the royal family, she remained true to her Benton, Illinois, roots. No one ever mistook her for a Brit.

She continued to call Margaret several times a week, not only to discuss food but to get her opinion on all the events of the day. Did Margaret think it was all right that she'd chased the Queen across Ascot in order to get a better look at her? She was afraid she might never get another chance. And what did Margaret think of her dreaming about Lord Mountbatten two weeks in a row? Did she think it *meant* anything, and should she tell Charles?

Margaret said that all things considered, it was probably best if this time Tusie just kept her mouth shut.

The Decorators

ONE

*B*ut getting back to that house of mine, the one with the café au lait chair, the space-age lamp and the big glass windows. I never did get around to fixing it up because almost immediately we had had to build an addition. In rapid succession four more children had arrived, and it seemed more prudent to put our money into square footage than interior decor.

The living room was now more than twice as big as it had been, the kitchen and family area almost triple. A wing with more bedrooms and baths jutted out from one side, an oversize playroom got the crunch out of the kitchen. I had finally succeeded in getting the space I needed, but inside the ambiance was still early Salvation Army.

Never mind. It was nothing that a healthy infusion of money wouldn't fix, and the help of a professional decorator. And as it happened that's just what Margaret's house needed too.

It all started one day when Mac said, "I think we should have separate bedrooms."

Mac and Virginia had always had separate bedrooms (probably due in part to how poorly he slept and his love of making coffee at 3:30 in the morning), and Mac saw no reason not to continue this arrangement. There was only one problem. Neither of the bedrooms available was very roomy and they shared an even smaller bath.

Separate bedrooms for virtual newlyweds? This wasn't exactly what Margaret had envisioned.

"Perhaps," Mac went on, hoping to soften this suggestion, "we should renovate the upstairs. After all there's no one living here any more except us. If we tear down some walls at the end nearest the stairs we'd have enough room to make two large bedrooms, each with its own bath, and I think we'd each be much more comfortable."

The possibility of doing over the upstairs made the idea of separate bedrooms more appealing; and the thought of a new bedroom with its own large bath designed especially for her was too good to turn down. Ever since Margaret had moved into Mac's house, there had been changes she had wanted to make; but Mac was resistant to all her ideas. Besides, he said, he was allergic to decorators.

Anyone who has lived in a house for a long time no longer sees it the way it really is. The large discoloration on the living room rug made by Fritz, the beagle, whose spot it was to sleep, made the room look "homey" to Mac. If Margaret didn't like it, she could toss an Oriental throw rug over it. The paint peeling off the fireplace didn't bother him at all. If you had fires every day, which he did, you had to expect some wear and tear. As for those water streaks on the aging wallpaper, left over from a leak in the roof, he felt they gave the room a "lived in" look.

If she played her cards right, Margaret thought, the renovation would give her a golden opportunity to consult a decorator; and perhaps, little by little, without Mac even realizing it, she could begin making changes in the rest of the house.

Margaret needed to put her stamp on the house, make it feel more like her own. Mac had let her plant daffodils and lilies of the valley along the woodland paths, and rejuvenate the two perennial borders, but the house still felt like another woman's house.

It was almost a year before the structural changes upstairs were complete. But at last it was finished and the business of making the rooms beautiful was finally at hand. The carpenters were done, the painters ready to start. It was time to consult a decorator.

TWO

Dix Hills was no place to look for wallpaper.

The next week, Margaret borrowed Ed, Mac's company chauffeur, and went to New York for the day. Nancy McClelland, she had heard, was the place to find beautiful wallpaper. By the end of the day she had found several samples she loved.

A few weeks later, she borrowed Ed again and went back to look a second time. As she walked into the Nancy McClelland showroom, she noticed a tall, thin, elegantly dressed young man in a dark pin stripe suit showing samples to a client. His immaculately coiffed black hair showed streaks of premature grey around his ears and across his temples; and he had the delicate chiseled features of a young English lord.

Margaret busied herself looking around, and when the client finally left, she went up and introduced herself.

"I'm Michael Greer," he replied, in his soft southern accent. "How can I help you?"

The colonial farmhouse where she lived in the country, Margaret explained, needed some new wallpaper. She was wondering what he thought of the paper she had picked for her bedroom. It had overscaled cream-colored Victorian roses with brown velvet leaves and winding green stems; and she wanted it both for the bedroom and the bath.

"Whadda ya doin picken out huge cabbage roses for a lil ole Long Island farm house?", he asked her. "This is very sophisticated paper!"

Margaret laughed and said she thought it would actually look very good indeed and would he care to come out and see the house for himself? It just so happened she might need paper for some of the other rooms too.

Michael said he thought that could be arranged. And picking out several more papers for her to take home and try, he said he'd do his best to get out to the country the following week.

Margaret was thrilled. The more they chatted, the more certain she was that she and Michael Greer saw eye to eye. What's more, she adored the way he seemed to be brimming over with stylish ideas for doing over the entire house.

He was the kind of person she'd have to keep as far away from Mac as possible.

THREE

The next week Margaret persuaded Angus and Ranny to schedule some meetings in the New York office so Mac would be busy in the city the whole day. Then she invited Michael Greer to come to the country and see the house.

Michael rented a car and drove out late morning, arriving in time for lunch. Even if it hadn't been lunch time, Margaret would have served food. Where she came from, nothing of importance transpired in life unaccompanied by food.

After giving him a quick tour of the house, they sat down to a delicious cheese souffle and green salad, with hot rolls and iced tea. And for dessert (no meal was complete without dessert) some homemade brownies and orange sherbert.

"What you need in this room are some important pieces of furniture," said Michael, surveying the living room after lunch, "and a new rug. This one's a disgrace." Margaret already knew that; the problem was getting Mac to know it.

"And while you're at it, you should do something about those curtains. In a room like the living room, they should come to the floor, not the window sill. Too cottagey, you know? The room needs a more formal feel." He picked out a sample from one of the papers he'd brought and tacked it up on the living room wall. Immediately the room felt more elegant.

"And the furniture ought to be reupholstered too. That fabric's a little too Betsy Ross."

This was going to be expensive.

By focusing Mac's attention on the decorating of his own bedroom and bath and offering to pay for the embellishment of her own, Margaret thought perhaps she could soften his attitude toward doing over the living room. The direct marketing company that Mac had started with his two sons was doing very well, and she didn't see any reason why they couldn't spend some money on the downstairs.

The clients now included Readers Digest, Time-Life, Book-of-the-Month, Bankers Life & Casualty, the Ford Motor Company and many other lesser lights. One whole floor had been leased for office space in the new Seagram building on Park Avenue, and Marcel

Breuer, the cutting-edge modern architect, had been retained to dress up the Westbury, Long Island plant. Space had been leased in Rutland, Vermont; Chicago, Illinois; Mt. Pleasant, Iowa; and Canada.

Recently Mac had mentioned wanting to give a series of dinner parties for some of the company's more senior executives. Margaret knew that Mac was a big believer in the power of entertaining, both clients and personnel; and as the head of a growing organization, she would tell him, it was very important to present a proper image.

That night after dinner, long after Michael had left, Margaret brought up the subject of the living room.

"With all the entertaining you're talking about doing, you really owe it to yourself to fix the house up," she declared brightly. "After all, the living room is the first room everyone is going to see."

Mac didn't say anything.

"Why I can just see the Prophets and the Lyons coming in and raving about what a beautiful house you have, and how pretty everything looks and how good the food is and what a great company it is to work for and . . . " Mac began to look more and more pleased with this rendition of his beautiful lifestyle and finally had to agree that viewed this way, perhaps she was right.

Before he could change his mind, the living room walls were repapered and the furniture recovered. An English breakfront was bought for the wall opposite the fireplace. The soiled green rug vanished, along with the beagle, who providentially died, and a delicate cream-colored rug took its place. At the windows were hung matching long cream-colored curtains banded with the same soft red and green of the newly upholstered chairs. Antique Lowestof and Tole lamps were purchased, the floral china ones retired to the upstairs bedrooms.

The room looked radiant. As a final gesture on his last visit out, Michael moved all the pictures on the wall down about a foot.

"Pictures should be visible from a seated position," he proclaimed, "not standing up."

A few nights later Angus and I stopped by to see the finished room. Mac was sitting morosely by the fireplace looking like he'd just been diagnosed with stomach cancer.

"Everything looks gorgeous," we enthused, wondering at his sour mood. "You must be thrilled!" He guessed it looked all right but then of course there was nothing wrong with it before. Anyway it was too late now, the damage had been done. But, he added, menacingly, you could bet your bottom dollar that was the last time he'd ever let a decorator in his house.

"They're all nuts," he said, pointing at the wall. "Why just look what that idiot has done. He's gone and moved all my pictures down so that now only Peter can see them."

Peter was his black standard poodle, who stood about two-and-a-half feet high. He had a limited interest in art.

In short order, as she knew he would, Mac forgot completely about the room as it used to be, and graciously accepted compliments on its present incarnation. He practically forgot that he had ever let a decorator into the house, acting as though the rooms had always looked this way.

FOUR

Meanwhile, up on the hill, I was having decorating troubles of my own. Our lively, burgeoning household now consisted of five children, a wild rabbit, two cats, a black lab, an indeterminate number of gerbils and two itinerant basset hounds who received Christmas cards from neighborhood families we had never met.

A little over a year after our son Sandy's birth, Katy was born, followed three years later by Jim. A year and a half after that Betsy was born, followed in three years by our third daughter, Anne.

Our house looked the way all houses look with small noisy children and assorted animals. The labrador was cutting his teeth on the dining room table, the cats were sharpening their claws on the upholstered chairs. The children launched themselves from the coffee tables and rocketed from the sofas onto the chairs. As for the color scheme, there wasn't any.

At first I was oblivious to the mess. When you have small children, you don't expect Architectural Digest. But as the years went by, I began to yearn for something a bit more elegant. The house was still modern, but with two-story windows facing north and south, cold bluestone floors and dark wood ceilings, the house had all the warmth and charm of a medieval dungeon, especially at night.

One day as I was driving Sandy and his new friend Kip home from school, Kip entered our house for the first time and said, "Cool, Sandy, I didn't know you lived in a Howard Johnson's!"

That's when I decided I needed a decorator.

"Who helped you do your house?" I asked the only person I knew who had more children than I did. Tusie's daughter-in-law, Anne Boone, lived in St. James where she was raising five children of her own, one step-child and one nephew. She even had more animals than I did, but her house had a warmth and an easy charm that I coveted.

Armed with her decorator's name, I called and asked if she would care to come over and look at my house. She said she would be over the following week.

The next Wednesday she arrived; and after I had given her a tour of the house, I served her lunch. Margaret said it was always best to serve decorators lunch. After wolfing down two large helpings of chicken salad and three glasses of wine, she thanked me and said she would be in touch.

After two weeks had gone by and I hadn't heard anything, I decided to give her a call one night after dinner.

"Hi," I said, "this is Bobbie McIntyre. You were over at my house a couple of weeks ago and I wondered what you thought."

There was a long pause. Finally she said, "Well, you come into the front hall and all you see is a blank wall; then you go into the living room and you see another blank wall; and then you look around and there's the worst assortment of furniture I've ever seen in my life. Frankly you ought to start by throwing everything out."

At the other end of the phone I was reeling. I had persuaded Angus that we had to spend a little money to fix up the house, but throw everything out? "Well thanks," I finally gasped, "I'll think about it."

Not knowing whether to laugh or cry, I hung up the phone and called Margaret. I was practically in tears. "You would not believe what she said," I wailed, giving her a blow-by-blow of the conversation. "It was humiliating!"

"Oh pay no attention," said Nana, "she was just drunk again."

I let a few months slide by before I summoned the courage to enter the decorating fray once more. This time I decided to call the Old Family Friend who did decorating on a part-time basis; presumably I wouldn't find her so threatening. I let her buy me a living room rug and make a few minor changes and then, since I had been reading up on decorating, I asked her if she was a member of the A.I.D., short for the Association of Interior Designers. I had heard that all the good ones were.

"What's the A.I.D.?" she said brightly. Besides, my daughter Betsy had overheard her say to her assistant one day, when they thought they were alone in my house, "Why in the world would anybody paint a library *this* color!" "*This*" was a soft green glaze that had recently been applied by a master painter. I decided it was time to move on.

"I tell you what," Margaret commiserated a few days later, "why don't I suggest to Mac that he pay Michael Greer to come out for the day and you can pick his brains. I'm sure he would do that," she said, "and if you like I'll come sit in on it."

I said that was the best idea I'd heard in months; Margaret got along with decorators like they were her long lost cousins. "Good," she went on; and then, getting down to essentials, she said, "Now let's plan what you're going to have to eat."

The following week Michael Greer arrived, walked in my front door and without a moment's hesitation announced, "You needn't worry. I love it." I was giddy with relief.

While I disappeared into the kitchen to fix lunch, Margaret started quizzing Michael on where Babe Paley was eating lunch these days. What exactly did she eat for lunch, anyway, Margaret wanted to know. Did he have any idea? It was hard to believe she ate anything more than a lettuce leaf, given how thin she was.

And why, she went on, didn't Mrs. Whitney have rugs in her summerhouse. She'd seen a picture in a magazine recently of the room and the floors were bare. Margaret thought all rooms looked better with rugs in them, even garden rooms. Of course one thing that had been bothering her lately was why Mrs. Vanderbilt didn't go to the racetrack any more. Did Michael know if something had happened to her?

Margaret didn't know any of these people, she just knew about them, and she was quite sure that Michael would too. Michael's star had risen swiftly in the years since he had done over Mac's house, and he now decorated in only the loftiest circles.

When I finally returned with a platter of grilled ham and cheese sandwiches and a pitcher of homemade iced tea, the conversation had turned to the flower arrangements at La Grenouille, its fabulous menu and where all the beautiful people were eating nowadays.

All during lunch we talked about food and what the best New York restaurants were and then Margaret wanted to know if it was true what everyone was saying about the ex-Governor, Nelson Rockefeller. Michael thought he did have a girlfriend, Margaret said she knew damn well he had a girlfriend and I said I didn't know what they were talking about.

The conversation went on like that until finally Michael looked at his watch and said he really ought to be getting back to town. "But what about my house," I cried, "we haven't talked about a thing!"

"Ahhh, your house," he replied. He made a few sweeping suggestions: "Get more color in here; buy a few good pieces of furniture; do something about that bare wall; get rid of the dining room furniture" —and swept out the door. His suggestions soundly oddly familiar.

The next decorator I tried was the Local Professional. He didn't know Margaret, he didn't like to gossip and I didn't have to serve him lunch. Besides he had done some work for a friend of mine that I'd admired. Perfect. There was only one problem. He wasn't any good.

Angus has never taken anything too seriously in life, me included. And at the top of his list of things not to take seriously was interior decor. My adventures in the decorating wars were simply one more source of amusement to him, something else to poke fun at. As long as he had a comfortable chair to sit in, a nearby table to put his beer on and a big enough bed to sleep in, all his decorating needs were met.

But seeing that I was genuinely upset, he stopped making bad jokes and tried to sound more solicitous.

"Listen, why don't you put your decorating plans on hold for now and wait for the children to grow up. In a few years, you know, they'll all be away at school and that would be a perfect time to get the house fixed up. In the meantime, why don't you start playing tennis again? Exercise is good for you."

Perhaps he was right, I thought. Decorating could wait. I could take up tennis, join an exercise class, find a new hairdresser or even embark on a total makeover. With my youth vanishing as swiftly as my waistline, my mid-forties looming right around the corner, maybe it was more important to do *something* about my looks. And the way things were going, there wasn't a moment to lose.

As Margaret liked to say, there was nothing worse in this world than a woman who had Let Herself Go.

Margaret as a young woman

Margaret, a young bathing beauty

The family, 1961. Back row l. to r.: Aden, Helen, Ranny, Sally, Angus, Bobbie. Middle row l. to r.: Sara, Sandy, Mark, Dinny, Katy, Maggy, Archie. Front row l. to r.: Susannah, Betsy, Jim, Mac & Annie, Margaret, Evan.

Mac touring the place in a golfcart with Mark & Sandy

The woodpile picture: Eight McIntyre grandchildren who grew up on the Place, 1961

The kids, l. to r.: Annie, Sandy, Katy, Jim & Betsy

Thanksgiving, 1970. Back row l. to r.: Angus, Mark, Sara, Maggy, Archie, Dinny, Ranny. Middle row l. to r.: Sandy, Katy, Margaret, Helen, Sally, Bobbie, Jim. Front row l. to r.: Betsy, Evan, Annie, Susannah.

Margaret in front of the Big House

1965—Margaret, Aden, & Louise

The Driveway into Hunting Hollow Farm

The Stable

The Big House

Our modern house

Margaret at Sally's house in Montecito

Tusie & Charles

The weddings: Dinny & John

Sandy & Carol

Maggy & Owen

Archie & Nina

Katy & Hakan

Sara & Kees

Thanksgiving, 1982—Helen & Margaret

Thanksgiving, 1984—Sandy's wife Carol and great-grandchildren Duncan & Sally

Looking Good

ONE

Step One on the rocky road to beauty was to find out what Nana used on her skin. Here she was, a senior citizen so high mileage she refused to tell her age, and her skin didn't have a single wrinkle. I was sure she knew something that I didn't and all I had to do was worm it out of her.

Every day whether she was going anywhere or not Margaret put on full make-up. This consisted of foundation, powder, blusher, eyebrow pencil, mascara and a nice bright shade of lipstick. When she had finished dressing for the day, she put on perfume, usually Joy. Her only concession to not going anywhere or seeing anybody was to leave off her corset.

As often as not the only beneficiaries of this effort were the delivery men or the help, since social life on the farm was mild to nonexistent. But that didn't matter to her in the slightest. Making an effort with your appearance was simply what one did. It was as automatic as brushing your teeth.

Despite mountains of evidence to the contrary, I have always believed implicitly in miracles. Find me that one miracle product and all my beauty problems would be solved. My chronically overstuffed bathroom cupboard has always been a glaring testimonial to the powers of cosmetic hype, a visible confirmation that given a good enough story, I could be persuaded to buy almost anything. Show me a jar that says "Age-Defying Complex" and I can't rest until I have it.

Nana had skin like a schoolgirl, even though she claimed she did nothing to it. All she did, she said, was wash her face with soap and water at night, and wear make-up during the day.

"There's no such thing as a cream for this and a cream for that," she told us. "Believe me, I was a Ziegfeld Follies girl and I can tell you right now that all anybody ever used was Pond's Cold Cream."

I always found that hard to believe and concluded that her good skin was probably due to her training on the stage. People in the theater world, I suspected, had some kind of inside knowledge.

"So what kind of make-up do you wear?" I asked. We were sitting on her porch one lazy summer afternoon drinking iced tea and complaining about the heat. Now that I had stopped worrying about the house, I was having a major anxiety attack about my looks.

"The same kind as Barbara Walters."

"Barbara Walters? How do you know that?"

"I read it somewhere, I forget where. Probably in the Enquirer."

Nana read the Times in the morning and the Post, Star and Enquirer in the afternoon. There wasn't much that she didn't know. What she didn't read in the papers, see on television or hear on the radio, she made an educated guess at. Actually it wasn't so much educated as visceral. She knew the ex-Governor had a girlfriend before the Enquirer did; the facts, she said, just didn't add up.

But getting back to make-up, both she and Barbara Walters looked gorgeous, I said, and what kind was it?

"Revlon, I forget what kind. Touch and Glow I think—I've been wearing it forever."

"Maybe I'll get some too," I said. "It really looks good on you." I'd only been looking at her for umpteen years, but suddenly I was noticing that she had fantastic skin.

Later that evening I was telling Angus how great her skin looked.

"She's got a fat face—that's why her skin looks good," he said dismissively. "It's kind of like a balloon with all the air still in it."

"Well I think it's more than that," I huffed, "and I'm going to buy some Touch and Glow just as soon as I can."

The next week I was in Bloomingdales buying sheets and checking out the Ralph Lauren department. Remembering the talk about make-up I went downstairs to the Revlon counter and asked to see Touch and Glow.

"Is it for yourself, honey?" said the saleswoman.

I said it was.

"Well we don't recommend that for anyone over twenty-five. Come on over here and I'll show you what I have for the more mature skin."

The day this happened Nana was crowding seventy. And I was in my early forties.

TWO

Nana's basic rule of thumb was that you owed it to yourself and to those around you to look your best at all times. When one of our daughter Betsy's boyfriends came roaring up our driveway one summer afternoon on his Harley Davidson motorcycle, sporting long dirty hair and a fu-manchu mustache, Nana turned to me and said, "My God, how'd you like to wake up and see that on your pillow?"

In her mind there was no excuse for not making an effort. Once when I took her to the children's school to watch the annual Christmas pageant, she pointed to a friend of mine and said, "Bobbie, why does that girl look like that?"

"Like what?"

"Like that! With that awful stringy hair pulled back that way and no make-up on and those terrible clothes. Why her husband should never have let her out of the house."

"Well, actually she always looks like that. Her husband must like her that way. Anyway she doesn't seem to care. She's a wonderful person," I added lamely, as though somehow that made up for it.

Nana just snorted. "She shouldn't let herself go like that. I think it's simply terrible." Letting Yourself Go was right up there with Bad Food.

She didn't like the way the headmaster spoke either.

"Why is that man mumbling so? I can't understand a word he says. He should learn to speak properly."

"I should have left you home," I hissed. What I didn't add was that she was also getting hard of hearing, but of course wearing a hearing aid was out of the question. Nana wouldn't even put on her glasses in a restaurant to read the menu. She'd look at the menu, and say, "What are you going to have?" Once you told her, she'd say, "Oh that sounds good. I'll have the same."

But if make-up was the sine qua non of the day, hair was the motor that drove the week. All other considerations paled around getting her hair done.

"Bobbie, do you think Rose got my hair too light this week?"

Rose was Nana's hairdresser, and getting the color correct was an ongoing concern. It must have been an inexact science, because one week Nana was sure her hair was too dark, the next week she was just as sure it was too light. To my eyes it never varied, still the same becoming reddish-blonde color it had always been. She wore it styled smoothly, with never a hair out of place.

Nana's weekly hair appointment was as much a social occasion as a beauty routine. Rose worked out of her own house and served tea and some sort of homemade sweet to her ladies, all accompanied by a running commentary on the news of the day delivered at the top of her lungs.

When Nana asked her one day if she was going to buy a certain house that she'd been looking at, Rose replied, "That building's so decrapitated I wouldn't live there if you paid me. Actually I've been thinking of selling my house and getting a condom." Another time when they were discussing celebrities, she yelled, "Don't you just hate that Jackie Kennedy? She always has to be in the lamplight!"

THREE

Nana was forever trying to get me to go to Rose. My unkempt hair became one of her ongoing missions. There was no reason in this world, she felt, why I couldn't be made as sleekly well-groomed as she was.

"It's a pretty color, Bobbie, but you should really do more with it. If you went to Rose every week it would make all the difference."

I had tried to explain to her that getting my hair "done" would be fighting a losing battle, that by the very next day it would look exactly as it had before it was done. I had the kind of fine slippery hair that wouldn't hold a set, and there was no point in wasting my money.

"I tell you what," I said one day, eager to put an end to this conversation once and for all, but equally eager to upgrade my image.

I had just finished reading a breathless article in Vogue about a famous New York hairdresser, named Mr. Edward. Wearing a navy double-breasted banker's suit, his few remaining hairs perfectly coiffed around his head like a latter day Julius Caesar, he presided, Vogue burbled, over a lavishly appointed salon just off Fifth Avenue. He had achieved god-like status in the firmament of trendy hairdressers and was said to do magical things with the hair of movie stars and presidents' wives. I was sure that if this paragon could ever do my hair, I would be instantly transformed. A miracle would occur. Besides, he had been quoted as saying that should you ever not like what a hairdresser is doing to you, just get up and leave. He sounded like my kind of man.

"I'll book an appointment with Mr. Edward," I said. "I've been reading about him in Vogue and he's the biggest thing to hit New York since Fiorello LaGuardia. It'll be my big splurge for the year. I promise you, you'll be thrilled."

Nana looked skeptical. She couldn't understand why anyone would go to New York to have her hair done when Rose lived just a mile down the road.

But finally she said, "Well, as long as you're going to New York I might as well go too. I'll get Mac to give us Ed and the company car for the day so we can go in style."

It took me three months to get an appointment with the exalted Mr. Edward and nearly that much time to save the money. By the time Nana and I drove into town she had almost forgotten why I was going. Her mind was preoccupied with buying new clothes for the spring opening of the racing season at Belmont and for once she wasn't thinking about hair.

Stanley Marcus, the head of Neiman-Marcus, who was married to her cousin Billie, had set up an appointment for her with a personal shopper at Bergdorf's. According to Stanley, all she would have to do is sit comfortably in a private room while clothes were brought to her. She wouldn't have to walk a step.

All the way into town we chatted about what I thought she needed to fill out her wardrobe and what were her most becoming colors. As we got ready to go our separate ways in the city, we agreed to meet for lunch at the Metropolitan Club at 1:00.

I too was in a state of anticipation. With so many children and activities in the country and the difficulty of finding a good babysitter, I hardly ever got to New York anymore. And I had never in all my life been to a name hairdresser.

At a little before 11:00 I climbed the stairs to the chair where Mr. Edward cut hair. I didn't want to keep anyone so illustrious waiting a single moment, though as it turned out there had been no one before me. I was his first appointment of the day.

As I walked toward his chair, smiling broadly, I saw his eyes glance at me quickly and glaze over. Stop being paranoid, Bobbie, he's probably looking at someone else. But when I looked around, there was no one else in his line of vision.

Relax, I told myself; there's no hope he's going to confuse you with Jackie Kennedy or Lucille Ball, but there's no reason you can't still get your hair cut.

I took a deep breath and sat down. "Good morning", I ventured, when nothing seemed forthcoming.

Dead silence.

I could see Mr. Edward in the mirror looking vaguely around the room, hoping to spot something more inspiring. But when nothing materialized, he finally turned toward me and asked "So, what are we doing today?" He still hadn't smiled or established eye contact or asked me my name.

Now when faced with going to a hairdresser, given a choice I'd rather go to the dentist. The dentist drills my tooth, fills it and I'm out the door. Maybe there's a little pain after the Novocain wears off, but there's a certain serenity in knowing I won't have to wait six months to be recognizable.

The hairdresser is another story. In the first place, he has an unfair advantage; he's the one with the scissors. This immediately puts you on an unequal footing from the start. Like a hijacker on an international flight, if this authority figure holding the weapon doesn't like you, you might as well call it a day.

The vibes emanating from the Great Man were not reassuring. He had obviously concluded I was neither beautiful nor famous. He most certainly could sense that I wasn't rich. And my hair was nothing to write home about. Altogether a non-person.

"I have difficult hair," I finally mumbled. "I was hoping you could cut it so I could manage it more easily."

As my hair started to fall around me like rain, I added, "If it's too short then I really can't manage it."

Holding up the scissors for a moment but still not really looking at me, he said, "Perhaps you see something that I don't see."

"Well, I just thought I'd mention it" I added apologetically.

I suppose this was the moment when I should have gotten up and left, the way the article in Vogue had suggested, but I only slid further down in the seat.

Five minutes later, half my hair was on the floor and what was left was being styled.

When I left the salon thirty minutes later, there was a damp mist rolling in, a veritable London fog. The midtown area was congested with traffic that was barely moving, so I opted to walk the ten or so blocks to the Metropolitan Club to meet Nana. She was going to be thrilled when she saw me. I had finally gotten my hair professionally styled, even though I was financially and emotionally ruined.

She was already sitting at a table wolfing down rolls and butter when I got there. "I shouldn't be doing this," she said enthusiastically, buttering another. "I just bought three new outfits and my stomach is sticking out a mile. I swear to God, everything I eat looks good on me." She took a big drink of water to wash down her roll.

"Wait till you see my outfits; they're *divine*! From now on this is the way I'm going to shop. You just sit there and let them bring you clothes. This Miss Whatsername, Stanley's friend, was absolutely *marvelous*! She knew exactly what I wanted. You're going to have to go and let her fix you up too. Oh, and I also looked at fur coats. I thought maybe I could get something on sale this time of year. Of course, Mac says a fur coat will just make me look fat, but I think I'm going to buy one anyway with my own money."

She rattled on about her new clothes and how becoming they were, and then suddenly I saw her looking at me quizzically.

Finally she said, "Now Bobbie, when is it you go to see this Mr. Edward?"

"I've just been, for God's sake, can't you tell? It cost me a hundred dollars!"

The damp mist and a ten-block walk had done its work. My hairdo was gone with yesterday's news, my ill-conceived cut hanging all over my face.

Nana began to laugh. She laughed until the tears rolled down her face.

"For God's sake get a grip," I snarled. By this time she was guffawing.

Finally she blew her nose. "You see," she said, still gasping for breath and wiping the tears from her face. "I told you you should have gone to Rose."

FOUR

A week later on a warm Saturday morning in May, Margaret and Mac were getting ready to go to the Turf and Field Club at Belmont Racetrack, their usual spring activity. It was a perfect day to wear one of the new Bergdorf outfits.

Nana loved getting off the farm for the day and going to the races. It was the one bit of social life that Mac seemed to enjoy, though if the truth were known it wasn't the people he was interested in seeing.

Mac was already dressed and anxious to get going. He was sitting in his favorite leather chair on the porch smoking a cigarette, drinking coffee, and drumming his fingers on the table beside him. He wished Margaret would hurry up. He needed to get to the track early enough to buy the Racing Form and three tip sheets so he could figure out the Daily Double for the day.

Finally he heard her coming. "C'mon, let's go," he said, "we're late already."

"Ohhh," she breathed, stepping gingerly down the step from the living room to the porch. "I'm so dressed up I can't stoop or squat. Don't I look divine, Mac?"

"Listen," he grumped, as he got up to precede her out the door, "at your age all you can hope to be is neat and clean."

PART THREE

Life on the Farm: Horses and Holidays

ONE

*M*ac loved to tell the story about the young man who showed up at a riding stable one day to rent a horse. "But I should point out to you," said the nervous young man to the owner, "that I've never ridden before." "That's not a problem," replied the owner, "we've got just the horse for you: He's never been ridden!" The story always made Mac laugh because he knew better than most people that a novice horseman and an unschooled horse had no business getting together.

It was clear from the very beginning that neither Margaret nor the daughters-in-law were going to learn to ride. As far as I was concerned, horses were best viewed from a discreet distance. The thought of getting up on one was about as appetizing as entering the Indy 500.

Mac adored horses. They were to him what food was to Margaret: the love of his life.

Mac's equestrian education began in Benton. Starting with his father, a country doctor, who made rounds in a horse and buggy, Mac had been around horses most of his life. But it wasn't until he moved to New York and was making good money with Charles Williams Stores that he was able to afford one. The first one he bought was a chestnut saddle horse named Chief; and because he was still living in the city, he stabled it in Jamaica, Queens.

Once he had the farm, he was seldom without horses again. Almost entirely self-taught, he learned how to judge at horse shows, how to school hunters, and in particular became an expert in horse conformation. Horse conformation is the science of how a horse should look and Mac had an unerring eye for it. He also knew there was good money to be made with a good-looking horse, if you knew what to look for.

One year on a hunch he bought a horse named King in upstate New York and entered him in the Piping Rock Horse Show's Model Hunter class, a beauty contest for young horses. No one at Piping Rock, an exclusive North Shore Long Island country club, had ever heard of Mac, but that didn't matter at all. Out of fifty thoroughbreds entered in the class that day, all of them outstanding, King won.

By the time all the grandchildren started arriving, his own riding days were long over. A lifetime of too many falls and too many improperly set bones had left his legs badly crippled. As long as I knew him, he walked with a cane and a large elevated lift in his left shoe.

The grandchildren re-energized him and the activity at the stable; he wanted them to learn how to ride. Now that he had the money to indulge himself, he bought four hunters named Molly, Roger, Top Fox and Dolly; four young racehorses named Poor Pebble, Cousin Katy, Stormy Outlook and Nobody Much; and a brood mare in foal. He then hired a groom to do the work.

With the help of an architect, he added a small tack room to the back of the stable, complete with a working fireplace, a small icebox, and big sunny windows facing the hastily constructed riding ring. It was a perfect place to sit and drink coffee on a cold winter day and watch the horses work out.

Now that the business was being run more and more by his sons and the younger executives, Mac had more spare time, and he thought he could have some fun training a young horse for the racetrack. His groom, as it happened, had a trainer's license, so between the two of them, he thought they could pull it off. They decided to begin with Stormy Outlook.

During the day, the young horse was trained on a lunge line and accustomed to the feel of a saddle. Then, when he was thoroughly used to a jockey being aboard, he was taken to Belmont racetrack and put through his paces. Mac loved nothing better than to go to the track before the sun came up and watch the horses work out in the early morning mist. Dressed in his houndstooth jacket and tweed cap, a pair of binoculars slung casually around his neck, he looked every inch the horsey country squire.

Stormy Outlook never distinguished himself. He consistently finished out of the money and eventually was shipped upstate to the Finger Lakes, dropped down in class and entered in a claiming race. When the race was over, he had been claimed for $7,500, $2,500 less than Mac had paid for him. But as they say, that's horse racing.

For pure entertainment though, nothing beat going to the racetrack on a sunny afternoon and playing the horses.

The racing season on Long Island started officially in the early spring with the opening of Belmont racetrack. It lasted until the end of July, at which point the racing world went to Saratoga. Almost every weekend during the spring and early summer, Margaret and Mac went to Belmont for the Saturday races. But it was Saratoga in August that Margaret loved best.

For Margaret, Saratoga was a real vacation. There were no meals to plan, no marketing to do, no help to supervise. She adored the huge old Gideon Putnam, where they always stayed, with its spa, its thermal baths and its full-service beauty salon. If only they'd known a few people she'd have enjoyed it even more. Mac never cared whether they knew anyone or not; he came to see the horses.

One hot August day, when hardly a breath of air was stirring, Margaret and Mac arrived at their Saratoga box to begin the day's racing. As she took her seat, Margaret noticed out of the corner of her eye that a very attractive man was seated in the adjacent box. He was wearing a blue and white seersucker suit with a yellow paisley tie and straw boater and he seemed to be all alone.

Shortly after they settled themselves, and had started reading their racing sheets, the gentleman looked at Margaret and said in a decidedly upper-crust accent, "So what do you like for the Daily Double?"

Margaret turned toward him, looking as though she'd just this instant become aware of his existence, and giving him her best Ziegfeld Follies smile, said she just couldn't make up her mind. "But," she added, fanning herself with her tip sheets, "it better be a horse that doesn't mind the heat; it's too hot to put one foot in front of the other."

He laughed and said he had a horse running in the second race, but he wouldn't advise her to bet on him. "So far this year he's finished out of the money every time."

Mac didn't like a lot of conversation at the track. He found it distracting. It prevented him from focusing on his Racing Form, his tip sheets and the changing odds up on the big board. After a cursory nod and a terse comment to their neighbor, he turned his attention back to his work.

All week long, the oppressive heat continued. And every day the debonair gentleman appeared in his box. He was always alone and happy to socialize. He and Margaret chatted away the afternoon, gossiping and exchanging racing information, fanning themselves with their tip sheets and enjoying themselves hugely. Mac ignored them.

Finally Saturday morning dawned bright and clear. The sultry heat of the previous week had disappeared in a clatter of thunderstorms the night before, and the air was cool and invigorating. It was a perfect day for the running of The Travers, Saratoga's equivalent of the Belmont Stakes.

Watching Margaret get dressed to go to the track, Mac eyed her narrowly, through a haze of cigarette smoke. Granted it was the day of the big race, but even so she seemed to be taking an excessive amount of time with her make-up and her clothes. All morning long she'd been in the beauty parlor having her hair and her nails done, while he, Mac, had sat in their room drinking coffee, chain smoking, bored out of his mind. Now she was trying to slide her dress slowly over her freshly done hair, so as not to disturb a single strand.

"Mac," she said, once the dress was safely down, "do you think my gold jewelry or my jade jewelry would look better with this dress?" She was wearing a becoming green and white silk print with a matching sweater and bone shoes.

She held the jewelry up to her face and appraised herself in the glass.

"Well now, why don't you just wear it all," he said, flicking his cigarette ash onto the floor, "the gold and the jade both. Then you can be all decked out like a Christmas tree and be the prettiest one." "Oh Mac," she said, looking at him quizzically, trying to read his tone.

"But I'll tell you one thing," he went on, catching her eye in the mirror, "if you don't quit flirting with that fella sitting next to us, we're going to have to go right home!"

When you're pushing seventy, Margaret thought, as she smiled delightedly back at her reflection, that's the kind of remark that can make your day.

TWO

In the fall, after the racing season was over on Long Island, long before it had started again in Florida, Nana focused her attentions on Thanksgiving and Christmas. Since she had the help and the space, she always volunteered to have the holiday dinners at her house. Her generosity probably sprang less from the milk of human kindness than her sure knowledge she'd eat better that way.

Given the amount of food involved, September wasn't a moment too soon to start discussing her Thanksgiving menu, even though it never varied from one year to the next. As the holidays drew closer, she began making a flurry of lists.

"You would not *believe* how much butter they want me to get." "They" referred to William and Janie, whose job it was to cook the meal, and who had been making this same meal for over ten years.

Margaret had walked over to my house to have afternoon tea. She wanted some cookies and couldn't find anything in her cupboard except saltines.

"Five pounds. Five pounds of butter for fifteen people. How could we *possibly* use that much?"

"Easy. The whole meal is always swimming in butter. Did you know that William's the only person I ever heard of that fries bacon in melted butter?"

Margaret laughed. "Well that's why it tastes so good."

The preparation of the food for Thanksgiving dinner took weeks. Everything was made from scratch, and since William and Janie preferred working at a leisurely pace, nothing else got done.

It took almost a whole day to french the string beans and another day to peel the little white onions. Bread was toasted and onions and celery chopped and fried in butter for the homemade stuffing. Sweet potatoes were baked for the sweet potato casserole and later whipped with butter and cream. Pastry was made for three kinds of pies. Apples had to be peeled, mincemeat made and pumpkins cut. Chocolate sauce was made for the homemade vanilla ice cream, since the younger children wouldn't eat pie. By the time the big day finally arrived the cooking in the household had reached a frenzied crescendo.

It was a feast to remember. The giant turkey that perfumed the house glistened on the sideboard, fat with stuffing. And around it, like so many beads in a necklace, lay all the trimmings. It looked as if it would take hours to eat, the turkey, the stuffing, the gravy, the rice, the sweet potatoes, the string beans, the onions, the hot rolls, the pies and the ice cream. But in fact it was all gone in a flash.

The family, fifteen to twenty strong, attacked the dinner like the starving Armenians we had all been raised on, all thoughts of manners, waistlines, diets or decorum out the window. No one waited for anyone else to be served, no one even waited for William to ask the blessing. By the time he did ask the blessing, the meal was half over.

The smaller children ate olives and dessert, the older children nothing but turkey and rice and dessert. The grown-ups ate too much of everything. In a stupor of satiation, the family at last retired to the sunporch to have coffee and more mints.

"I think I'll go home and take a nap," said Aden, looking like he'd just emerged from a subway gassing. Aden, Mac's cousin, always celebrated holidays with us, since he had no family of his own. "I can't stand the noise," he said.

"What noise?" I said, puzzled, so inured to the cacophony of small children that I no longer heard it.

"I think I'll take a nap too," said Nana. "My corset is killing me. I probably shouldn't have had that fourth piece of apple pie."

Mac had already gone upstairs to lie down and recover. Only the children had gotten their second wind.

THREE

In the winter, after all the commotion of Christmas had come and gone—the planning, the shopping, the visiting, the decorating, the cooking, the eating and the endless number of presents—Margaret and Mac went to Florida to recover. And to get away from the winter.

In Florida, there was no snow and two racetracks: Gulfstream and Hialeah. For two or more months during the worst of the winter, they settled comfortably into a luxurious Miami motel on the water, blessed with a heated pool, a first-class restaurant and individual haciendas complete with kitchens for those who preferred to cook.

William went along to do the cooking.

A week before their flight, William drove south with all the luggage, arriving in time to meet their plane and help them get settled.

Once there, he fixed their breakfast in the morning; and in the evening, if they didn't feel like going out to dinner, he cooked. Since William loved going to the racetrack and also despised snow, he too considered Florida a vacation. Besides he had relatives near by.

The days had a predictable rhythm. In the mornings, after a leisurely breakfast, Margaret took her daily exercise swimming in the pool. She didn't actually do laps; she just kind of splashed around in the shallow end, gingerly swimming the sidestroke from one side to the other so as not to get her hair wet. Then she and Mac got dressed and at noon William drove them to the track.

Once at the track they had lunch and studied the tip sheets. Then they placed their bets for the daily double. Some days they stayed for all eight races; some days, if they hadn't slept well, they left early. At night they occasionally ate out, but most evenings they were happy to let William cook.

One morning, after they'd been there for a few weeks, Margaret woke up and said she felt dizzy. Margaret had had her first heart attack a few summers back shortly after Ranny and Helen's son Mark had been thrown by a horse. Mark had only had a mild concussion, thanks to the hard hats that all the children wore, but in the excitement of watching him be rushed off to Huntington Hospital, she had experienced her first serious chest pains. Ever since, the occasional dizzy spells that plagued her had made her very nervous.

"I think maybe I should see a doctor before I go to the races today," she said to Mac at breakfast. "I'm sure if I call the front desk they'll be able to recommend someone." An hour later, a rather elderly Dr. Wilson appeared at the door of her hacienda.

Dr. Wilson took her temperature, her blood pressure and her pulse. They were all normal. Next, he listened to her heart. Normal too.

Then he said he wanted to test her reflexes.

Taking a small hammer-like instrument out of his bag, he tapped her gently, first on her knees and then on her ankles.

Then he said, "Close your eyes and open your eyes." She closed and opened her eyes.

"Now raise your right hand. Raise your left hand." She lifted both hands in the correct order.

"Touch your shoulder." She did. "Touch my shoulder." This was a piece of cake.

"Now pull your ear." She pulled it. "And reach and pull your toes." She reached forward and gave his nose a good yank.

"Jesus," Dr. Wilson yelled, leaping to his feet and looking like he'd just encountered a certified loony. "I said *toes*, Madame, not nose."

With a long sigh, he leaned over and put his instruments back in his black bag.

"I cannot find anything wrong with you, Mrs. McIntyre, nothing at all. But let me suggest that the first thing you do when you get back home is have your hearing checked."

Mac and Margaret never made any money at the track; that wasn't the point. They never lost very much either. They went because it was an entertaining way to spend the day and Mac liked being around horses. It gave Margaret a chance to get dressed up, get out of the house and see some people. Besides, she said, the Turf and Field Club had the best rolls and butter in the world.

Sometimes they invited us, sometimes they invited the grandchildren. I once won $100, the only money I ever won in my life, on a horse called SanKaty, a hunch bet I made when I had too much trouble reading the Racing Form. It turned out to be as good a method of handicapping as anyone else's.

Nana hated losing money at the racetrack. If she got more than fifty dollars down during an afternoon, she'd quit betting for the rest of the day. In fact after she had her first heart attack, it gave her palpitations just to watch a race if she had more than twenty dollars riding on the nose.

When she did have a bet in excess of twenty, she'd excuse herself just before the starting bell and go to the ladies room. Once safely inside where it was hard but not impossible to hear the moment-by-moment public address system, she'd stick both fingers in her ears and say to anyone who happened to be in there, "What's happening, what's happening? Who's winning, who's winning?"

Socializing

ONE

Every year, sometime around mid-December, when New York was festooned with a million lights, Margaret and Mac and whichever of the eight Long Island grandchildren were deemed old enough to go piled into the company limousine and drove to New York to see the sights. Ed, the company chauffeur (or Ed, the Talking Horse, as the children called him), was behind the wheel.

Going to see the sights meant driving down Fifth Avenue at twilight to see the holiday windows and the tree at Rockefeller Center; then looping back up Park Avenue to see its long string of Christmas trees and decorated office buildings; and then cutting back toward Fifth Avenue again at 59th Street. Eventually the car would come to a stop in front of F.A.O. Schwartz, the world-famous toy emporium.

As soon as Ed had turned off the motor, the children would explode out of the back of the Cadillac and burst through the door of Schwartz, scattering in eight different directions with Nana in hot pursuit. This was their one big chance to see the toys they could wish for on their Christmas lists and give Santa Claus some expensive ideas. Since Mac could hardly walk, never mind run, he preferred to stay in the car with Ed.

"Children! Not so fast! Stay together! Nana can't keep up! Children *please!*"

She might as well have been talking to some deaf mutes, for all the good it did her. It was like letting eight mice out of a rat trap.

Of all the children our younger son, Jim, was far and away the slipperiest and the hardest to catch. And the most determined to go his own way.

"Jim, slow down, you're going to give me another heart attack. And then I'm never going to take you again," Nana added. But Jim, already a seasoned veteran in the school of empty threats, would just ignore her and race full speed ahead for the trains upstairs.

Somehow or other, with the help of amused onlookers, all the children got rounded up after an hour or so and stuffed back into the car. Then it was off to Aden's apartment on the Upper East Side for a dinner of hamburgers, potato chips and ice cream and a magician with a bag load of tricks. Aden, who had no children of his own, enjoyed entertaining ours.

One year, after the party had become an annual event, there was a great deal of discussion about whether Archie was old enough to go. Archie was Helen and Ranny's youngest child and the year he turned three it was decided he could go. He was an easy and well-behaved child and everyone agreed he would be no trouble at all.

On the drive into the city, Ed the Talking Horse was feeling expansive. Mac didn't like Ed to talk while he drove, sensing correctly that he drove better when he kept his mouth shut. But Ed had just bought a boat and couldn't contain himself.

Ed was a car person and had never owned a boat before, so he was somewhat perplexed about how to describe the boat's sterling qualities.

"It goes very fast," he bragged, eager to impress the children. "Like a rocket, in fact." The children didn't say anything.

"I would say it goes at least a good twenty miles an hour." The children didn't seem impressed.

"What's so good about that?" said Mark, who knew even less about boats than Ed.

"Well, of course that's in the water," said Ed, as if to imply that it went even faster on dry land.

"Ed, you better pay attention to where we're going or we'll never get there," said Margaret. And Ed, sensing that he'd talked himself into a hole, ended the conversation.

The evening went perfectly. New York was dazzling in its Christmas finery, F.A.O. Schwartz had an even more elaborate train setup than the year before, and Aden's cook put on such a wonderful feast that the children went back for seconds and even thirds. Archie took everything in stride.

But later that night on the drive home Archie turned to Nana and said, "I don't feel very good." A minute later he turned toward our daughter, Katy, and erupted all over her brand new camel's hair coat.

"Ed, pull over to the side of the road and stop for a moment," yelled Nana.

Grabbing Archie by the arm, she pulled him out of the car to get some fresh air. By this time five-year-old Katy, a shy, serious little girl with big green eyes, was starting to cry over her soiled new coat. "My mother's going to kill me," she blubbered.

Meanwhile the other children were all yelling about the terrible smell.

But it wasn't until Ed got out of the car to spit up a little too that Margaret broke up. All the children were either crying or yelling or throwing up, the chauffeur was throwing up, and there was Nana, all done up in her new fur coat and her new fur hat standing alongside the car on the Grand Central Parkway, with snow on the ground and stars in the sky, laughing her head off.

TWO

An enjoyable social life on the farm was always problematic for Nana. She loved people and people loved her, but there was almost no one in the neighborhood who was exactly her cup of tea.

There was Barbara across the road, who could be counted on to bring her poodle over for afternoon tea. But Margaret didn't particularly enjoy having her for lunch or dinner because she took too long to eat.

There was Mrs. Leeston-Smith, a devout Christian Scientist who had been a friend of Mac's first wife, Virginia, but Margaret found that a little of Mrs. Leeston-Smith went a very long way.

Margaret was a Christian Scientist too, but primarily when it suited her. The lessons of Mary Baker Eddy discussing the effects of the mind on the body comforted her after her first heart attack; but as far as going to church was concerned, she preferred to stay home. As for doctors and medical advice, she wanted the very best.

Other than that, there was no one, although occasionally Rose, her hairdresser, would come over for tea if she didn't have a client.

One of the time-honored ways to meet like-minded people in a new community is to volunteer. But charity work just wasn't Nana's bag. She couldn't get worked up about it. It wasn't that she had no social conscience; she had enough empathy for all of Long Island. It was simply that she liked her charities close to home and personal.

The plight of the homeless or the problem of unwed mothers, the refurbishing of public gardens or the future cure of macular degeneration meant nothing to her. Too general. Too amorphous.

It was Crystal's problems in Benton that attracted her attention: Crystal who had been married to Margaret's alcoholic brother, Bob, and was now nursing a dying second husband with no help and almost no money. And later, much later, it was Janie's problems after she retired: Janie who had cooked all that mouth-watering Southern food for her and who was now back in Aiken, suffering from diabetes and failing eyesight. It was Crystal and Janie who got her attention and what money she could spare, not some big charity she didn't understand.

And then of course, there was the problem of Mac. No matter how you sliced it, Mac was antisocial. Aside from family—*his* family, not Margaret's—he didn't care if he ever saw anybody. Business entertaining was one thing; it helped you sell accounts. But entertaining people for the pure sake of socializing was at the bottom of his list.

Margaret enjoyed socializing. People amused her and energized her. And she loved nothing better than a good party; in fact she was usually the life of it. But when I introduced her to some of the mothers of my friends on the North Shore, nothing ever really took.

I could never figure out whether it was interest-related or age-related. The traditional North Shore enthusiasms of bird-watching, Planned Parenthood and the Nature Conservancy left her comatose.

And when you got right down to it, so did most people her own age. It was our generation she loved. Ours and the next one down.

Margaret loved to gossip. She liked to talk about books, the theater and the movies; about clothes and make-up; about houses and decorators and household help and relationships. People were what interested her, not causes. Occasionally she liked to discuss politics, but usually individuals, not issues. She was a liberal and a Democrat, not a popular position on North Shore Long Island.

But nothing got her juices flowing like a good red-hot scandal, the more outrageous the better. Angus always said she viewed life like a spectator at a bullfight: The more gore that got splashed around, the better she liked it. Nana liked people who were entertaining and amusing. You could skip the worthy.

One early spring day, after I'd been living on the farm for almost fifteen years, my friend Janet London called and said she wanted to have a luncheon. She said her garden had never looked more beautiful, bright with tulips and pink dogwood, and she wanted all her friends to see it. She thought she'd invite her mother, who lived near by, our friend Olivia and her mother-in-law, and me and Margaret, a two-generation party. We would be six altogether.

Janet was a wonderful cook; everything she ever made was superb. So I knew, if nothing else, that Margaret would enjoy the food. It seemed a golden opportunity for Margaret to meet some genteel contemporaries in a pleasant and relaxed setting and perhaps even find a new friend.

The morning of the luncheon Margaret called to say she thought she'd wear her new tweed skirt with the matching Fair Isle sweater that she'd recently bought at the Hitching Post in Cold Spring Harbor. I assured her they would be perfect.

And because she didn't think tweeds and Fair Isle sweaters were quite dressy enough, she was going to add a Hermes scarf, her gold beads and some large gold earrings.

After she had dressed and put on her make-up, she went to Rose to have her hair combed out. At noon when I picked her up, she looked the perfect picture of a stylish, well-to-do North Shore matron.

As it turned out, she could have saved herself the trouble. The two other grannies, as she later pointed out, were straight out of the American Gothic school of beauty, two Grant Wood look-alikes minus the pitchforks. No lipstick, powder or make-up of any kind had ever darkened their collective brow. Their hair was exactly as God had given it to them, now an indeterminate shade of grey. And their clothes brought to mind the old story about the Boston dowager who when asked where she bought her hats replied, "We don't buy our hats, we have our hats." The grannies' outfits had probably been in their closets since the first world war.

I glanced at Margaret and I could tell by the look on her face that she didn't think this was going to be a whole lot of fun.

During lunch, the conversation was light and inconsequential. We talked about gardens and food and houses and grandchildren. Janet had made a delicious chicken curry salad with grapes, which she served with iced tea and warm French bread. And for dessert (Margaret was thrilled she was going to get dessert), she had made raspberry ice cream and rich shortbread cookies.

After lunch, we all went outside to have coffee and mints in the garden. It was a lovely spring day and Margaret seemed to be truly enjoying herself. I was relaxing back in my chair thinking what a nice party it had been, when Mrs. Kramer spoke up and said, "That Lyndon Johnson is the most terrible President."

Next to me I felt Margaret snap to attention.

It was 1965, the start of the escalation of the Vietnam War, and all over the country Americans had begun to protest.

"Well, he certainly is, the old fool," said Margaret jumping in with both feet. "They say he has his hand up every skirt that passes by. In fact they say he's been cheating on his wife for years, and old Ladybird just ignores it and looks the other way."

This wasn't precisely what Mrs. Kramer had in mind. In fact it was probably the farthest thing in the world from her mind. Mrs. Kramer was congenitally straight-laced. Her beatific smile, a smile that seldom left her face, told you that she took the greatest pride in never saying anything bad, *really* bad, about anyone.

"Speaking of Ladybird, I have a cousin in Benton," said Margaret warming to the subject, "who says she can never remember Ladybird's name. She always refers to her as Lilypuss. She says that anyone called Ladybird deserves to be called Lilypuss."

Margaret laughed delightedly thinking of Lilypuss, but the two other grannies just looked nonplussed. They had no idea what she was talking about.

"Johnson's really no better than Jack Kennedy," Margaret concluded, "though Heaven knows Kennedy was a lot better-looking. I don't have a life-size picture of Marilyn Monroe jumping into bed with Lyndon."

The conversation started to wind down from there and pretty soon everyone got up to say goodbye. I knew Margaret would want to get home and have a nap.

"That was a delicious lunch," I enthused on the drive home. "Didn't you think? Janet is really a terrific cook."

"Grapes have no business being in a chicken salad," said Margaret. "But I thought the dessert was good." Then thinking she ought to sound more enthusiastic, she added, "She really did put the big pot in the little one. It was a very nice luncheon."

We drove on a little further before I asked, "So what did you think of them, the two other grannies?" I knew perfectly well what the answer would be.

"Welllll."

"Well, what?"

"Well, they weren't a whole lot of fun."

"Yes, but didn't you think Mrs. Kramer was nice?," I asked, baiting her some more.

I could see her starting to laugh. "Why yessss indeed, I thought she was just as nice as she could be!"

By this time we were both laughing.

"But if you really want to know," Margaret said, "she made me think of what Poppa used to say about Cousin Mary, a sanctimonious old fool if ever there was one. There she'd be every Sunday singing her heart out in the church choir just like she had a direct line to God. Poppa'd turn to my mother and whisper—Maude, that woman wouldn't say shit if her mouth were full of it."

Sex, Marriage and Grandchildren

ONE

*N*ana never gave us advice, unless of course we asked for it. "With my daughters-in-law," she always said, "I tread very lightly." But we never had any doubt where she stood on all matters large and small. Take marriage, for instance.

Considering she'd never been married before, Nana had very firm ideas on how a marriage should work.

Her two rules for a successful marriage were:

1. Don't ever go away in the summer and leave your husband alone.
2. Don't ever have anyone in the house (help, that is) who's prettier than you are.

She thought sex was great, fooling around not so great. "And if you want your marriage to last," she cautioned, "you'd better go to bed when your husband goes to bed; because if you don't, somebody else will."

Sex, Nana told us, was what drove the world; everyone was either doing it or wished they were. The sooner we understood this, the better off we'd be. As for feminist rhetoric, it fell on deaf ears. Her Momma, whose loving marriage had lasted until "death do us part", let her husband go on believing his whole life that he was the center of her universe, even on days when he was not. Women who ignored this basic rule of common sense probably got what they deserved.

Nana was as comfortable with sex as she was with a peach cobbler and just as enthusiastic. Growing up I had never heard the word S-E-X mentioned. If there was something men and women were doing to produce the children in their lives, my nervous parents hoped I'd find out about it at the movies.

Her easy, earthy attitude sprang from the healthiest self-image I ever encountered. "My pretty, sweet Margaret", her mother had called her and the message had stuck. She had beautiful skin and a radiant smile, but if you took her features apart, they were nothing special. Her face was too full and her nose too big. Yet she projected the image of an extremely attractive woman, even into her seventies and eighties. When she walked into a room everyone looked up. At a bit over 5'9" you couldn't miss her.

Her figure was womanly, with large breasts and almost no behind. Though she was always slightly overweight and planning to diet as soon as she got around to it, she liked herself the way she was.

"I just hate these big things," she'd say patting herself on the chest and smirking at her modestly endowed daughters-in-law. It was clear she didn't hate them at all.

"My brother Bob always said about Tusie and me—watch out all you bird-watchers, here come a couple of Big Titters. And then he'd poke us in the chest with his elbow and make us cry." The implication was plain that any woman less endowed than Margaret would never stand a chance with the opposite sex.

The rest of her sexual equipment she referred to as "Ol' Possible."

"I have to go into New York next week and get "Ol' Possible" checked out", she'd say. "I've been going to the same ob-gyn for *years*."

"Old what?"

"Ol' Possible. You know. Down *there*."

"That's what I thought you said. Why in the world do you call it that?"

She laughed. "I've called it that forever. Down home we used to have a hired girl working for us while I was growing up. Her house had no indoor plumbing, so on Saturday nights she took a bath standing up in a little galvanized tub. One day the fella that cut our lawn asked her how she got clean in such a small space.

"'Well,' she said, 'first I washes up as far as possible and then I washes down as far as possible.' He thought for a minute and then asked, 'Well what do you do about ol' possible?'"

Nana laughed delightedly thinking of "Ol' Possible" and said, "So I've called it that ever since."

TWO

That Nana enjoyed the company of her daughters-in-law was no great surprise. There was almost nobody else around.

But her relationship with her grandchildren was an ongoing miracle. Growing up on the farm were Helen and Ranny's three—Dinny, Mark and Archie—and our five—Sandy, Kate, Jim, Betsy and Annie. If you had lined the eight children up in front of a woodpile, which we did, and put a board on their heads, which we did not, it would have made a perfect slide.

In California, meanwhile, Sally was raising the remaining four: Maggy, Sara and Susannah, and her son, Evan. In ages and size they would have fit in perfectly with the group in front of the woodpile.

Nana was hardly your garden-variety grandmother. She didn't baby-sit, or cook, or play games or do sports. She couldn't sew and she couldn't knit. She didn't help with homework (she told the children she'd gotten a zero in math) or take the children to the movies. As far as I know she never wrapped a Christmas present or a birthday present; the housekeeper did it. In fact she didn't even buy "her" presents for the children; she "preferred" to let us do it, so she got it "right."

Having never had children of her own, it was anybody's guess how Nana would take to having grandchildren. But from the start it was a mutual admiration society all around. They adored her, all twelve of them, the eight living on the Place and the four growing up in Santa Barbara. She had a consuming interest in the minutiae of their lives, and they reveled in the attention.

In the beginning, when she thought maybe she should be doing something grandmotherly, she decided to teach the grandchildren to perform. In Benton it had been customary for the young to entertain the grown-ups on Sunday afternoons by singing songs and playing musical instruments. Now she decided she would teach Dinny and our daughter, Katy, to do the same. But when they sang "Aura Lee" for her one day: "Aura Lee! Aura Lee! maid with golden hair, sunshine came along with thee, and swallowed up some air," she decided not to pursue it.

Matters of discipline she was happy to leave to us; Nana couldn't even discipline her dog. But the one area where she did try to exert some influence was at the pool.

"You better pick up your bathing suit," yelled our daughter Betsy at one of her friends, "or my grandmother will give you a black mark!" Black marks were a dreaded threat that never materialized, but the threat was enough to keep the pool area moderately tidy.

As the years went by, the children didn't hesitate to ask her advice about their friends and later their lovers; about their clothes, and about their hair; about smoking and drinking and partying; about parents and the ways of the world. When they asked her how she knew what she did, she just laughed and said that at this point in her life, there wasn't anything she hadn't seen. They had no reason not to believe her.

When they were convinced that their parents were impossibly archaic, she could put things in perspective, give the advice they didn't want to hear from us. And by managing to convince each one that he or she was the apple of her eye, she became privy to the most astonishing information.

As the children got older she took a particular interest in their love lives. If she couldn't learn what she wanted from one, she'd just quiz one of the others. Since she had a genius for asking leading questions, she was in on almost everything that went on, often before we were.

One year when our son Sandy was interviewing at hospitals for his medical residency, he spent the night with his cousin Dinny, Helen and Ranny's tall, beautiful daughter, who was living in Cambridge, Massachusetts pursued by an army of admirers. On his way back to California, Sandy stopped on Long Island for a short visit and Nana invited him to tea.

After she'd asked him how he was and how he liked California and if he had a new girlfriend, Nana cut to the chase.

"Now Sandy, there's just one thing I want to know. Is Dinny living with that fella, the new one she's been seeing, the one with the blonde hair?"

"How should I know."

"Well, was he there when you went to bed at night?"

"Yeah."

"Was he there when you got up in the morning?"

"Yeah."

"That's all I need to know," said Nana, her curiosity fully satisfied. "She is."

Another time when our youngest daughter, Annie, was home on vacation, Nana invited her to come have supper and watch "Dynasty", their favorite Wednesday night ritual. Annie was eager to talk to Nana and get her advice. She had a new beau at college, a tall handsome crew jock who called her regularly whenever they were apart, and she thought she might be in love.

This particular evening Annie and Nana were sitting on the porch having supper on a tray. Nana looked at her watch and said, "Whoops, we better turn the TV on, or we'll miss the beginning."

As Joan Collins' face swam into focus, they both settled happily back in their overstuffed chairs to enjoy the latest histrionics of Alexis and Blake Carrington.

Just as the dramatic tensions started escalating, the phone rang.

"Shit," said Annie.

"Hello?" said Nana, picking it up. And then, "Just a minute, please. Annie, it's for you, it's your fella."

"Tell him I can't come to the phone now," said Annie, totally engrossed in the ongoing drama. "I'm too busy."

"Well," said Nana, after she hung up, "You can forget about him. There's no way in this world that he's the love of your life."

Nana was for having fun. Her real area of expertise lay in sitting on her porch, preferably in the afternoon after she'd had her nap, and "laughing and talking." No subject matter was considered off-limits for "laughing and talking"; and most subject matter was explored in depth, a process called "getting into it." This was always accompanied by food, usually tea and homemade cookies.

The cookies Nana served, mainly butter cookies with walnuts or tiny chocolate bits on them, were a mainstay of the household, turned out continually by whatever cook was currently in residence and stored in round tins in the freezer. The only store-bought cookies that ever entered her door were made by Metrecal, a barely edible cross between a zwieback and a dog biscuit. Nana ate them when she was dieting.

With a crackling fire burning in the fireplace, good food to munch on and no parents around to interfere, Nana's porch was the perfect place for letting it all hang out. It was as much a part of the grandchildren's growing up as going to school. When our little red-headed daughter Betsy complained in the first grade that "Posy is my best friend and we don't get along at all," Nana just reassured her that that's usually the way it is with best friends.

"It's just like sisters," Nana told her, " or first cousins. When I was growing up Tusie always had to be the prettiest one."

When Mark was all grown up and living temporarily in the little white cottage next to hers, Nana's fun escalated by a factor of ten. Mark was Dinny's younger brother by a year, and had just graduated from college and entered the work force. His trials and tribulations as an eligible bachelor kept Nana on the edge of her seat.

"That girl," said Nana, inhaling a cookie and sipping decaffeinated tea, "is the fool of the world, driving down here every weekend from the Eastern Shore. She's making it too easy for you and you're going to get sick of her."

Mark had come over to chat.

"She should stay put, make you go down there and see her. Play hard to get."

"Well, it's more convenient this way. I'm busy."

"You'll see," said Nana.

A few months went by and sure enough the Washington girl had faded away and a new girl was now in the picture.

The new girl was local so she didn't have to do any long distance driving. What's more she seemed a cat of a different stripe, more determined than the previous one to define the relationship on her own terms. She was small and dark and sassy; and since Mark was currently in his shake-up-the-family mode, her different background just whetted his appetite.

And then one day, out of the blue, she lost her temper. Big time. It happened over Christmas, a mixup of some kind over presents, and it didn't even happen in person. Just over the phone. But the storm it created reverberated through the rest of the holidays.

"Well that's that," said Nana, calling to report what had happened. "You can bet your bottom dollar we've seen the last of her. This is not a family that solves things by yelling. On to the next one!" she laughed.

Occasionally, Nana's enthusiasms backfired. One year, when our son Jim was a junior in college, he asked if he could invite a girl he'd recently met to dinner. I said that would be lovely and what should I have to eat.

He said whatever I wanted to cook was fine with him, "but there is one thing, Mom, especially if you invite Nana. Before dinner all we ever talk about is what we're going to eat; during dinner all we talk about is what we're eating; and after dinner all we talk about is what we ate. Do you think just this once we could talk about something different?"

But perhaps Nana's finest hour came when Sara's marriage broke up. By this time, Nana was in her high eighties.

Sara, Sally's second daughter, had come east from California to work in New York. While waitressing at the Bottom Line, she met and married a young man in the music world, a free spirit unused to the confines of marriage. It was an uneasy alliance from the start, embracing a world of too many differences. When it finally broke up for the last time, Sara moved out to Long Island to stay with Nana. It was the dead of winter.

From Nana's point of view, it couldn't have been better timed. It was many years after Mac had died, and her help situation had gone from bad to worse. Since she no longer liked being alone in the house, having Sara around full time was the answer to a prayer. Sara could keep her company, shop at the supermarket, cook dinner and drive her to the hairdresser. In return, Sara would get her very own Ann Landers.

By the time summer finally came around, Sara was on her way to recovery.

It was the same summer that our daughter Katy was married in our garden to a young scientist from Sweden. Katy was a scientist too and had met her husband-to-be doing postdoctoral work in Boston. Since it was a "company romance" all the scientists that worked in both their labs were included on the guest list.

Sara, of course, was invited along with all the rest of the family. But the morning of the wedding, she balked. She wasn't sure she wanted to encounter the whole family trailing a broken marriage behind her, and she announced to Nana that she didn't think she'd go.

"Of course you're going to go," said Nana. "Katy would be very hurt if you didn't. And who knows, you might even meet someone. Now go put on something pretty. It never hurts to look pretty."

Sara went, and meet someone she did: a young Dutch scientist named Kees, who after spending the whole afternoon with her, begged her to look him up if she ever got to Boston. A few days later she did just that.

After a whirlwind courtship between Boston and New York, Sara and Kees were married in Holland.

"Wouldn't you know," said Sally, "that Sara would fall for the only guy at the wedding who wasn't wearing a tie."

And Nana said, "Well now we don't have to worry about that anymore."

The ongoing soap opera of the grandchildren's lives was a constant diversion for Nana. But it was always a two-way street. What the grandchildren got from Nana was a lifetime load of common sense and an unerring instinct for doing the right thing.

PART FOUR

Winding Down: The End of an Era

ONE

In 1967, Mac died of heart disease brought on by a lifetime of smoking.

Margaret lived almost seventeen years longer. It never occurred to her to do anything but stay where she was. She loved her house and she loved the farm. After almost twenty years, the Place was home. Besides with family around she had everything she needed.

Vinny continued to mow her lawn, plant her vegetable and flower gardens, fill the birdfeeders with sunflower seeds and bring pink geraniums onto the sunporch in the winter. "What in the world would I do without Vinny?," she said. "Vinny's my angel." And no matter where she went, she always said when she got back home, "Ours is the prettiest place in the whole world. No place else can touch it."

The fall after Mac died, Vinny got married.

Vinny and Ray Falkowski had arrived on the Place shortly after Angus and I had and never left. They came five days a week and did whatever needed doing. They cut the grass, grew the vegetables, planted the flower garden, cleaned the swimming pool, raked the driveway, trimmed the bushes, painted the fences, cut the hay, plowed the snow, split the wood and fixed whatever was broken.

Several times a month, when the work let up a little, they drove to Westbury and worked on the grounds of the McIntyre plant, to justify being on the company's payroll.

The Falkowski family were not matrimonial enthusiasts; in addition to Vinny and his brother Ray, six more unmarried brothers still lived at home, happy to let Mom and Pop keep doing what they had always done.

But now Vinny had decided to take the plunge. He was in his late forties and everyone said it was time. For his bride he chose one of the nurses who had cared for Mac during his final illness.

"What are you going to wear to Vinny's wedding?" Margaret asked on the morning of the big day. "I haven't been anywhere or done anything in so long I feel like getting dressed up for a change. I'm sick to death of tweed skirts and Fair Isle sweaters. Of course I don't want to overdo it, but I was thinking I might wear that brocade dress and matching jacket that I bought for that terrible Metromedia party we all had to go to. If I don't, I'll probably never wear it again."

"Sure, why not? It looks great on you. Why don't we pick you up around 3:15 and you can go with us." I knew Margaret was eager to get to the Towne House early so she didn't miss a thing.

The Towne House was a wedding mill on Jericho Turnpike that ran weddings with clocklike precision. You were ushered in when your time slot came up and ushered out when it was over. If your timing was off by even five minutes, you were likely to end up unmarried.

Angus and Margaret and I arrived around 3:30, in plenty of time for a 4:00 wedding. Margaret opted to sit in the third row of the small chapel where the actual ceremony would occur. She reasoned that with Vinny's large family she should leave the first and second rows free, but she still wanted a good seat. She felt we were Vinny's family too, just not his immediate family.

Margaret sat down and looked around. In her brocade outfit, her fur coat thrown loosely over her shoulders, a pretty veil on her freshly done hair and as much jewelry as she could pile on, she looked regal and elegant.

We had been sitting for about fifteen minutes, when a large group clattered in and filled up the first two rows. Right in front of Margaret a gentleman of generous proportions sat down wearing an ill-fitting suit and thick glasses. He kept mopping the back of his neck with a large checked handkerchief.

Pretty soon he turned around to see who was sitting in back; and looking up and down the row, paused at Margaret and smiled. Margaret smiled graciously back.

After a moment or two he turned around again, once more pausing at Margaret. Preening, she raised her chin in the air the way she always did when she wanted to smooth out her neck and minimize her jowls, and gave him her most dazzling Queen-of-the-Manor smile. Obviously he must know that she was Vinny's employer.

A few more minutes passed. Finally, he turned around a third time, and this time looking straight at Margaret said, "Say, ain't you Bertha Falkowski's cousin from New Jersey?"

TWO

Not too long after Vinny's wedding, William came down with prostate cancer. It was discovered by chance in a routine checkup. When the doctor asked him what approach he wanted to take, he replied, "If it don't bother me, I ain't gonna bother it." He then returned home and went about his life. He continued to cook for Margaret and take the poodle for walks in the afternoon. On alternate Sundays he preached in the Wyandanch Baptist church. He died in his sleep a year later.

After William was gone, Janie went back to Aiken, South Carolina. Her diabetes had worsened and her legs bothered her all the time. Her eyesight was failing badly.

None of the cooks that followed ever measured up. When the first cook to come after Janie tried her hand at a cheese souffle, it never even rose above the dish.

"It squatted to rise," Margaret reported disgustedly, "and got baked on the squat."

THREE

In 1975 Angus and I moved to Canada. The move was only temporary but it took us away for a number of years. Metromedia had bought the American McIntyre direct mail business to add to its growing media empire, but the Canadian division had not been sold. It was now in need of full-time attention, and with all our children away at school and college, this seemed the perfect moment.

Not too long after we moved, Margaret checked into University Hospital for an overnight stay and a biopsy of her colon. After she got back home, I called to see how everything had gone.

"It took two hours to get admitted," Nana complained.

"Good Lord, aren't hospitals the pits."

"They kept asking me all these stupid questions, Bobbie. And then they took my blood pressure and another electrocardiogram and more blood samples even though I'd just had all that done two days ago at home."

"Well I guess it's part of hospital admitting procedure. They like to run their own tests."

"They couldn't believe I'd never been in the hospital before. The girl kept saying–how can you be eighty years old and have had two heart attacks and never been in a hospital? I told her my doctor knew I'd get along much better at home. Then she said to me—what are you? I said, what *are* you–what do you mean what *are* you? Well, you know, she said, what are you? Why I'm a little widdee woman, I told her! She just looked blank, so I said I'm a widow. Helen was giving me a look that said we'll be here all day if you don't quit horsing around."

Helen was married to Angus' brother Ranny, and happily for Nana had not moved to Canada.

"And, Bobbie, you should have seen my room. There were five people in it. *Five*. There was this black woman right next to me who kept saying, 'If I was just home now, my husband would be bringing me two pork chops for dinner.' I told her that sounded awful good to me. You couldn't eat the food. It was kosher and didn't have any salt or pepper." She sighed loudly.

"Why didn't you put some salt and pepper on it?"

"You still couldn't have eaten it. Anyway, what with all the enemas and the laxatives and the horrible food I must be getting down to human size. I'm sure I've lost at least five pounds. Before I went in the hospital, my stomach was sticking out a mile."

"Did your neighbor eat her dinner?"

"Well, she sort of picked at it and then she asked me if I knew how to cook chicken backs. She said you had to cook them very slowly with rice and chicken stock and a little onion and lots of salt and pepper, and then let it all simmer for a long, long time. I think William and Janie used to cook chicken backs. I'll have to ask Janie the next time I call."

"I'm sure Janie would know. That's very Southern."

"And then there was this crazy woman two beds down. You've never seen so much make-up and she didn't know a thing in this world about how to put it on, I might add. Why she had enough on for the first act in a Broadway play! She kept complaining because she'd forgotten her hair dryer. She wanted her hair dryer and she wanted her operation. She said she'd come in five days ago for her operation and she still hadn't had it and she wanted her husband to bring her her dryer and her doctor to give her her operation. Her husband finally showed up around ten o'clock with her hair dryer and her doctor came by around eleven to calm her down; and then she turned on her TV until two in the morning."

"Lord, aren't some people impossible."

"I didn't sleep a wink, not a wink. They wheeled me into the operating room about ten the next morning. Reese was there and was simply marvelous."

Reese was Margaret's internist on Long Island.

"I didn't have any make-up on and looked like an absolute dog," she sighed.

"Maybe you should have borrowed some from Mrs. Crazy." I could hear her laughing.

"Well, they gave me a big shot of valium and Reese said it would make me feel very relaxed and sleepy and I wouldn't feel a thing. Bobbie, it didn't do a damn thing for me. I felt everything. I had no idea you could feel so much up your rear. While I was on the operating table I kept thinking of that book, you know, the one where the girl finds out her best friend is pregnant and has to get an abortion and she says to her, 'In the mouth or up the ass is fine, dear, but why on earth did you let him put it up *there*!'"

"You're terrible. It's a good thing the doctor didn't know what you were thinking."

"Well he was terrible too. Meanest little Jap you ever saw. I guess he's good at his job—Reese says he's the best—but he never said good day, goodbye or piss in your hat. I told Reese he could have used some of Reese's bedside manner. Reese says the doctor does eight or ten of these biopsies a morning and charges $800. for each one. Can you imagine? Eight hundred dollars! Why he must have so much money he can't even jump over it."

"That's probably why he's so mean, because he's so rich."

"Maybe I won't pay his bill—I'd rather give the money to Reese. I knew Reese was worried, Helen said he was worried. He didn't come right out and say I had cancer but I could tell that's what he thought and he was preparing me to know it. I thought, Isn't it just like me to get cancer for my birthday?!

"'At your age you have to expect things to happen, Mahhhgrett,' Reese said."

Reese had a slight English accent, which Nana adored.

"'Why lots of people your age don't even have their wits about them anymore and your mind is just as sharp as ever.' I told him that'd probably be the next thing to go."

Well, I thought, she doesn't have to wait for the test results. She knows already that she's got cancer. Reese knows it too, or at least he's 95 percent sure. Her symptoms were not reassuring.

"I'm amazed they let you go home so quickly."

"I am too. The doctor said I could leave right away and I told Helen I couldn't wait to get out of there. I'll bet they were awful glad to see me go," she laughed. "I tell you I've never been so glad to get home in my whole life."

"Do you want me to tell the children?"

"Well, whatever you want. Just say Nana got cancer for her birthday. Reese says it could be ten years before it bothers me and I said I'll take it. My heart will probably give out on me before that."

I could tell by the sound of her voice that she'd already put it behind her and was thinking of other things.

"Billie Marcus will be in town next week for a few days before she and Stanley leave for Italy. Did I tell you that Stanley's being honored by the Italian government for all the support Neiman-Marcus has given to Italian fashion? I'm wondering what I ought to wear when I go in to have lunch with her. If it stays warm maybe I'll wear my black linen dress with the white coat. Do you think that would look all right?"

"Perfect."

"I guess I'll take her to the Metropolitan Club. Did I tell you the last time I took somebody to lunch there it cost me an absolute *fortune*? But of course it's very comfortable and you can always get a table."

THREE

Now that Mac was gone, Margaret was free to travel. Not that travelling had ever been a great priority. But Nana enjoyed getting out and seeing the world and Mac never really did. Once when they were vacationing in Ireland, it had rained for a solid week, effectively imprisoning them in their cold, drafty hotel. After about the fourth day of uninterrupted downpours, Mac had turned to Margaret and said, "I'd give everything I own to be back in my own room and look up and see William coming down the hall with a pot of coffee." After that they never went anywhere again.

Now Margaret could go wherever she wanted; she had no one to please but herself.

"Why don't you go on a cruise?" said Daisy, who'd been married to Aden's brother and was now a wealthy widow. Daisy adored going on cruises. Her idea of a perfect vacation was dressing up every night in evening clothes, drinking scotch and socializing with strangers. But cruises didn't appeal to Nana at all. She no longer owned a bona fide evening dress and scotch gave her a headache. Besides, she considered vacationing with strangers a waste of time.

Travelling to Nana meant going to California to visit Sally, Angus' sister, and going to England to visit Tusie and Charles. Staying in hotels wasn't what she had in mind either.

"I think I'm going to be selling the house in Montecito soon and buying a smaller one in Santa Barbara," Sally said one Sunday afternoon during her weekly telephone call to Margaret. "You really ought to come out and stay with me for a couple of weeks while I still have it."

Sally's Montecito house was large and roomy, with plenty of extra bedrooms and baths and a heated swimming pool in the garden, so Margaret knew she'd be very comfortable.

"As a matter of fact, why don't you come out with Tusie and Charles?" Sally enthused, warming to the idea. "I'd have plenty of room for all of you, and that way you'd have more fun. You'd also have someone to keep you company on the plane."

As soon as they could get organized, Margaret, Tusie and Charles flew to California and settled in for a visit with Sally. Their days quickly settled into a routine.

Twice a week Sally took Margaret and Tusie to get their hair done. In between she took them shopping. They shopped for clothes and for groceries, for plants for the house and pottery to put them in. They went to lunch at the club and had lunch in the village. They visited vineyards and they visited gardens. Charles tagged along when it was outdoors or for lunch; but otherwise, exemplary Englishman that he was, he was happy to stride briskly around the neighborhood enjoying the warm California sunshine and getting his daily exercise.

One day, after they'd all been there for a while, Sally said she thought she'd have a luncheon. Through her mother-in-law, Bobbi Lewis, who also lived in Santa Barbara, Sally had met some of the older generation, and she thought Margaret and Tusie and Charles might enjoy meeting them too.

Bobbi Lewis had never really approved of Margaret, much to Sally's and Margaret's amusement. "You'd better watch out for her," she had warned Sally early on. "My stepmother made off with all the family silver." But for the most part she was pleasant and cordial.

"Now who all is coming?" Margaret asked over an english muffin and coffee the morning of the party. "You'd better tell me some of their names or I won't be able to keep it all straight."

Sally went over who was coming, giving their names and a little of their background. And then she said, "Oh yes, there's one woman who's a very good friend of Bobbi Lewis', but I can't remember her first name and I don't know anything about her. But you'll recognize her the minute she comes in—she looks just like Captain!"

Captain was Aden's Norwich terrier.

Margaret and Tusie spent the morning relaxing and leisurely getting dressed. Having had the foresight to get their hair done the day before, nothing was pressing them. Tusie put on a navy linen suit that she had just bought in Montecito, and Margaret wore a green silk suit with a plaid scarf that she had recently bought at Bergdorf's to wear to the races. Sally's helper arrived mid-morning and was busily preparing food in the kitchen. With all the bustle in the household, Nana forgot all about Captain.

Around 12:30, the guests began arriving, California ladies in brightly colored dresses and hurricane-proof hair. Sally skillfully performed the many introductions, never forgetting a single name.

And then the door opened and in came a small sturdy woman with a little pointed face and hairs sprouting out of her chin and under her nose. Margaret took one look and said, "Ohhhhhhh, my God!"

It was Captain incarnate, a Norwich terrier in a Doncaster suit and Ferragamo shoes.

The poor woman never could understand why Sally's stepmother whom she'd been invited to meet could barely shake hands, and why she was laughing and crying so hard she had to excuse herself and leave the room.

As far as I know, no one ever tried to explain it to her.

FOUR

Tusie and Charles continued to divide their time between England and the States. One year their visit to Long Island coincided with Christmas and we invited them to spend Christmas Eve with us. All the children were home and Annie was just getting over the chicken pox.

A few weeks later Charles came down with a sore throat and swollen glands and Tusie took him to the doctor. The doctor seemed perplexed. Finally he said, "This probably sounds silly, but have you ever had the chicken pox?" Charles was 76 at the time.

"Well," he said, looking puzzled, "I don't know. I'll have to ask my mother."

His mother was alive and well and living in England at the age of 98. She said he hadn't.

FIVE

Mac's cousin, Aden, continued to rent the red cottage on the road and to come out most weekends. He was closer to Margaret than anyone else in his life and they had always enjoyed each other's company. They both still liked going to the races on weekends, and Margaret, with her two heart attacks, was comforted having an eminent cardiologist on the Place.

But when Aden died unexpectedly (Nana had never thought she'd outlive him), his will produced a storm of outrage right up there on a par with the Watts riots. Aden made the very fundamental mistake of leaving his money to the wrong people.

Totally ignoring all the folk who had always been there for him, particularly Margaret, he cut a deal with his widowed sister-in-law, Daisy, a woman he could barely tolerate. Their bond was that neither one had any immediate family left to inherit money.

They agreed to leave their money to each other. The last one to die would then leave it all to Northwestern, where Aden had gone to medical school; it would be enough to endow a chair. And as if that weren't bad enough, the lawyer who drew up the will, a man no one in the family had ever heard of, managed to insert his two sons in the document as well. In a total breach of lawyerly ethics, he persuaded Aden to provide for their educations.

Margaret had what is known in our family as a Hard Fit. It is a Benton expression and it means a large volcanic explosion, the kind that keeps rumbling and reverberating long after the initial blast.

Nana was hurt, stunned and most of all mad. She had propped Aden up for so long. All those years, she had watched out for him, taken care of him, kept his housekeeper from quitting on him, found a cleaner for his Long Island house, had Vinny cut his lawn. And this was the thanks she got. Nothing. A big fat zero. And she could have used some extra money. Besides, the thought of that smarmy Daisy now sitting on top of all that money was enough to curdle her stomach.

Try as she would, she couldn't stop talking about it. Once a week or more she would bring it up, and then we would have to analyze Aden's will all over again. "Wills are the most terrible things," she would say, "they really hurt people."

Angus said Aden's will was like being bitten by your own dog.

SEVEN

Eventually, travelling got to be too much for Nana. When this happened Sally fixed up the little white cottage next to the Big House and did her visiting on Long Island. Mark was now long gone from the cottage, pursuing his bachelor's life in Brooklyn.

As the years went by, Margaret's television and telephone became her lifeline to the world. She usually sat on her sunporch in the big red leather chair that had always been Mac's, with her phone on the table next to her, the television directly across from her. Through the big glass windows she had a wonderful view of what was happening on the farm: who was riding, who was swimming, who had a girlfriend or a boyfriend and who was learning to drive a car. Sally said that if she could only find someone to throw a log on the fire, she'd never have to move at all.

Her days were spent talking (usually with Merv Griffin yammering in the background) to a regular network of people with whom she kept constantly in touch. Nana never could understand why anyone would spend good money going to a therapist. If you had enough family, she reasoned, you just called them one by one until you got the problem solved. Nana believed in involving, if not the whole world, at least the immediate world in anything that bothered her, even though her phone bill, she complained, looked like the national debt.

In the evenings during dinner she watched Archie Bunker in "All in the Family." She watched it with the same spirit with which she would have taken a drink of scotch. It relaxed her and made her laugh. And unlike scotch it didn't give her a headache.

When I asked her one day what she minded most about getting old, she said, "Well, besides my arthur-itis, as William always called it, it's that men don't look at me 'that way' anymore. The only ones that still give me the eye are the ones in wheelchairs."

Each month, and sometimes oftener, she got dressed up in her most becoming outfit, got her hair done and went to see Reese for a check-up. I never knew anyone else that thought going to the doctor was such a blast.

Handsome, urbane and witty and twenty-five years her junior, Reese practiced medicine in the old school. He knew instinctively that a large part of his ability to keep her well was inextricably tied up with her enormous fondness for him. And because he shared her interest in books and the theater, he always took the time to discuss what he was reading and tell her what plays he'd seen.

"Have you read 'The Girl in the Red Swing,' Mahhhgrett?" Reese asked her one day. "It's about the Stanford White murder—you'd *love* it!"

Nana always had several books going on her bedside table, usually biographies about someone in the entertainment field. The ladies at the library always knew to call her when something particularly juicy came in.

Finally, when her appointment was over, Reese would get up, walk her to the door and tell her how marvelous she looked and how much he enjoyed seeing her. No doubt about it: He added a good ten years to her life.

After she had her second heart attack, Reese insisted she get on a regime. He made her lose weight, improve her diet and get on an exercise program. He said he wanted her to walk a mile a day. Every day.

She bought some good-looking, low-heeled Ferragamo shoes with crepe soles and borrowed one of Mac's old canes. And sticking to the dirt roads and driveways on the Place, she managed to map out exactly one mile. It was the first time she had ever seriously put one foot in front of the other.

After a number of false starts, the grandchildren began settling down. Dinny, Sandy, Archie, Maggy, Katy and Sara all found the mates of their dreams and married. By the time Katy's wedding rolled around, there were four great-grandchildren.

Nana adored the weddings even though she found them exhausting. Her visit back to St. Louis for Archie's wedding was especially nostalgic, a trip down memory lane. She had a chance to see family that she hadn't seen in years and a city she had known since childhood. When Louise's son Bill, who was still living in St. Louis, had a brunch for all the out-of-towners the day after the wedding, Nana said it was the first time she had had any decent grits since William died.

In 1984 Angus and I went back to Canada for the last time. It was September and this would be our final winter. But because we decided not to rent our Long Island house, we told Nana we would be home for Thanksgiving. "I'll do it at my house this year" I volunteered, "all the kids want to come home. And please don't worry. After thirty years I know how to cook turkey."

It was a wonderful festive weekend with a large family turnout. The married grandchildren brought their spouses, the unmarried ones their boyfriends and girlfriends. And Sandy and his wife, Carol, who by this time had produced two great-grandchildren, brought the next generation.

The week following Thanksgiving, Angus and I returned to Montreal. A few days after we left, Reese put Nana in the hospital. She had been complaining of chest pains again and he didn't want to take any chances.

Over the next few days he kept a close eye on her, and when nothing further developed, he decided to let her go home. Delighted, Nana called Helen; and getting no answer, left a message on her machine. "Come get me tomorrow," it said. "Reese says I can go home. And please make an appointment at the hairdresser. I need to have my hair done." It was the last we heard.

Nana died that night in Huntington Hospital. She was 89 years old.

So what was her appeal? I guess it was family values, pure and simple. She adored her family and we responded in kind.

You could tell her anything and she never got her wind up or made believe she felt one way when she felt another. If she was upset about something, like Aden's will, you heard about it. Probably more than you cared to. But she never let a problem go unresolved.

She could be a snob, all right–she would have *loved* one of the grandchildren to marry rich and famous, giving her a year's worth of conversation–but she never pretended to be anyone she wasn't.

Once when I took her to the then most celebrated restaurant in New York, Henri Soulé's Pavillon, for a birthday lunch, she turned to the maitre d', a man of enormous self-importance, and said, "So where are all the sella-britties?" "I beg your pahdon, Madame?" he replied. "I came to see the sella-britties," she said again, and when he still looked blank, I finally said, "I think she wants to see some celebrities."

But she really never cared who you were or where your family came from or what your name was or how much money you had. She loved reading and talking about "sella-britties" and the super rich–it was her version of "Days of Our Lives"; but she also knew that money didn't care who had it and that a fancy lineage was just an accident of birth.

If you were fun and entertaining, she wanted to know you; she hoped you'd come for tea. And if you were related, so much the better. Nana saved her best manners for her family, not the stranger at the cocktail party whom she would never see again. No question about it, she could have taught Newt all he needed to know about family values.

It's hard to think that Nana's been gone more than fifteen years now. You'd think she'd never gone away, listening to us when we all get together, still telling the same old stories, still using the same old Benton expressions. It's as though they had become such an ingrained part of our lives, we were no longer able to think any other way.

Now, when I least expect it, I'll find myself thinking of her. Just last week Angus and I were in our lawyer's office signing wills and I started to laugh. Our lawyer must have wondered why I thought signing wills was such a laughing matter, but all I could think about was Aden's will.

Sometimes when I'm doing something else, I'll hear Nana talking to me. What are you going to have for dessert? I'll imagine her asking when I'm getting ready for a dinner party. And what are you going to wear? I can hear her saying when I'm getting ready to go out in the evening. And sometimes when I'm not thinking of her at all, I'll catch my reflection in a mirror and hear her say, "Now, Bobbie, when are you going to do something about your hair?"

Postscript: In 1995 the Place was sold to a developer who has put up fifty-five houses.

www.ingramcontent.com/pod-product-compliance
Lightning Source LLC
Chambersburg PA
CBHW030327080526
44584CB00012B/748